READY TO
WRITE MORE

FROM
PARAGRAPH
TO
ESSAY

KAREN BLANCHARD
CHRISTINE ROOT

 LONGMAN

Ready to Write More: From Paragraph to Essay

Addison Wesley Longman, 10 Bank Street, White Plains, NY 10606

Editorial director: Joanne Dresner
Senior acquisitions editor: Allen Ascher
Associate editor: Jessica Miller
Production editor: Christine Cervoni
Cover design adaptation: Naomi Ganor
Photo research: Polli Heyden
Text art: pages 40, 50, 70–71, 77, 86, 106, 110, Daisy de Puthod; pages 19, 23, 42, 69, 95, 139, Jessica Miller;
pages 1, 14, 24, 33, 53, 55, 85, 100, 116, 133, 135, 136, Jim Russell

Grateful acknowledgment is given to the following for providing illustrations and photographs: p. 3, reprinted
by permission: Tribune Media Services; p. 31, © Kindra Clineff MCMXCII; p. 62, reprinted by permission:
Tribune Media Services; p. 67, courtesy of New York State Department of Economic Development; p. 72,
© 1996, reprinted courtesy of Bunny Hoest and *Parade* magazine; p. 88, © Greenpeace/Beltra; p. 88, courtesy
of Pelham Historical Society, Pelham, NY; p. 88, courtesy of Publishers Clearinghouse; p. 89, © Robert
Visser/Greenpeace, 1993; p. 89, courtesy of the *Pelham Weekly*, Pelham, NY; p. 125, © Andrew D. Bernstein,
courtesy of the NBA; p. 129, by Steve Rossi, courtesy of Photo Run; p. 129, courtesy of Mrs. H. F. Heyden;
p. 130, "Watson and the Shark": Gift of Mrs. George von Lengerke Meyer, courtesy, Museum of Fine Arts,
Boston; p. 131, Wyeth, Andrew. *Christina's World.* (1948). Tempera on gessoed panel, 32¼ x 47¾"
(81.9 x 121.3 cm). The Museum of Modern Art, New York. Purchase. Photograph © 1997 The Museum
of Modern Art, New York; p. 137, drawing by Rini, © 1995 *The New Yorker* Magazine, Inc.; p. 137, Wiley
© 1996, Washington Post Writers Group. Reprinted with permission.

Text credits appear on page 152.

Library of Congress Cataloging-in-Publication Data
Blanchard, Karen Lourie, [Date.]
    Ready to write more / Karen Blanchard, Christine Root.
      p.   cm.
    ISBN 0-201-87807-0
    1. English language—Textbooks for foreign speakers. 2. English
language—Composition and exercises. I. Root, Christine Baker,
[Date.] . II. Title.
PE1128.B587 1997
808'.042—dc20   96-26254
                                       CIP

1 2 3 4 5 6 7 8 9 10–CRS–00 99 98 97 96

To the memory of Michael Blanchard:
for his enthusiasm toward writing and his enduring spirit.

Acknowledgments

We are grateful to several people whose contributions so strengthened this book. Thank you to Kathy Buruca and Robby Steinberg for their inspired suggestions for activities and to Alan Bronstein, Hasan Halkali, Leslie Leibowitz, Matthew Root, and Josh Rothbard for allowing us to use their essays. Thanks also to Dan Hogan and David Root, our management and technical consultants, and to Daniel Blanchard and Ian Root, apprentice editors extraordinaire. Finally, thanks to Allen Ascher, Christine Cervoni, Amy Durfy, Françoise Leffler, and Jessica Miller at Addison Wesley Longman for their perspicuity, creativity, and steadfast support.

Contents

Quick Reference Guide

Successful techniques for writing the introductory paragraph of an essay 42

Functions of a thesis statement 44

Successful techniques for writing a concluding paragraph 49

Editing 55

Introduction

Ready to Write More is a writing skills text designed for intermediate and high-intermediate students of English as a Second Language as well as native speakers who are ready to write more than paragraph-level pieces. It is intended to build on the fundamentals of paragraph writing that students learned in *Ready to Write* and to give them the confidence they need to venture into the realm of writing longer pieces.

Ready to Write More is based on the premise that because different languages organize information differently, ESL students need to be shown how to organize information in English if they are to write effective essays in English. Beyond that, students also need to understand that good writing is not necessarily a natural gift. It is a network of complex skills that can be taught, practiced, and mastered. The text teaches competency in these skills by taking students on a step-by-step progression through the processes that promote good writing.

The first four chapters of *Ready to Write More* comprise an overview of the building blocks of good writing: prewriting, the elements of paragraph writing, the basics of essay writing, and revising and editing. Chapters 5–9 present practice in writing five-paragraph essays of process, classification, cause/effect, comparison/contrast, and problem/solution. We recognize that many essays do not conform to the five-paragraph format but believe that it is helpful to students in that it gives them a structure that they can always fall back on. In Chapters 10 and 11, students practice writing summaries and personal expression, two essay styles necessary for Chapter 12, in which they complete a sample application and write essays for undergraduate and graduate school.

The activities in *Ready to Write More* are intended to help students become competent, independent writers by engaging them in the process of writing and by encouraging them to explore and organize their ideas in writing. Students are called upon to write often and on a broad range of meaningful, thought-provoking, and interesting topics. The tasks are presented in a clear, straightforward manner and lend themselves to ease of instruction. Incorporated into the tasks is a variety of follow-up personal and peer-revision activities. Although *Ready to Write More* is a writing book, students practice their reading, speaking, listening, and analytical skills as they progress through the text.

Two popular features from *Ready to Write*, "You Be the Editor" and "On Your Own," have been expanded and appear regularly throughout *Ready to Write More*. "You Be the Editor" provides effective practice in error correction and proofreading to help students monitor their own errors, especially those of the type presented in Chapter 4, Revising and Editing. An answer key is included for these exercises. "On Your Own" provides students with further individual practice in the skills they have learned. A new feature included in the first three chapters of the text is "Chapter Highlights," a review section that crystallizes for students the key points they will need to keep in mind as they work through the rest of the book.

We hope that you and your students enjoy working through this text now that they are *ready to write more*.

KLB and CBR

CHAPTER 1

Getting Ready to Write

Not everyone is a naturally gifted writer. Writing is a skill that can be practiced and mastered. In many ways, it is like driving a car. If you have ever driven in another country, you know that some of the rules of the road may be different. Just as the rules for driving differ from country to country, the conventions for writing may change from language to language.

Writing in a different language involves more than mastering its vocabulary and grammar. Language, including written language, is a reflection of the thought patterns of native speakers. In order to write well in a different language, it is important to understand the way native speakers of that language organize their thoughts. That is why it rarely works to write something in your native language and then translate it into English. The words may be in English, but the logic, organization, and thought patterns reflect those of your native language.

To write effectively in English, you must conform to the accepted patterns of organization. The exercises in this book will put you on the road to becoming a better writer.

Determining Your Attitude toward Writing

Your attitude toward anything that you do in life greatly affects your success in doing it. Writing is no exception. Think about your attitude toward writing **in your native language** as you complete the following exercises.

1. Circle the appropriate responses to the following statements about writing in your own language.

   Use the following scale:

   $$1 = \text{Strongly Agree}$$
   $$2 = \text{Agree}$$
   $$3 = \text{Neutral}$$
   $$4 = \text{Disagree}$$
   $$5 = \text{Strongly Disagree}$$

   a. I enjoy keeping a diary............................ 1 2 3 4 5

   b. I like to write letters to my family
   and friends... 1 2 3 4 5

   c. Writing about my feelings helps me relax.... 1 2 3 4 5

   d. I enjoy working on reports for school
   and work.. 1 2 3 4 5

   e. I enjoy writing personal essays. 1 2 3 4 5

   f. I like to write poems, stories, or songs......... 1 2 3 4 5

   g. I enjoy using electronic mail. 1 2 3 4 5

   h. I like to write for my school
   or town newspaper 1 2 3 4 5

   i. Writing is a creative outlet for me................ 1 2 3 4 5

   j. I feel good about my writing ability............ 1 2 3 4 5

2. Add up the numbers for each of your answers and divide the total by ten. Put that number in the box at the right.

3. The final number is your average score for the ten questions. Overall, it will tell you how much you like to write. The closer your score is to "1," the more you like to write. The closer your score is to "5," the less you like to write.

4. Based on your answers, what general conclusions can you make about your attitude toward writing in your native language?

_____

_____

_____

5. Write a paragraph about your general attitude toward writing.

_____

_____

_____

_____

_____

_____

_____

Small-Group Discussion

In small groups discuss your answers to question number 4 above and then answer the following questions:

1. What kinds of things do you enjoy writing about?
2. What types of writing does your job or future profession require?
3. What do you hope to gain from this course?

Elements of Good Writing: SPA

SPA is an acronym that stands for **subject**, **purpose**, and **audience**—three of the most important elements of good writing.

a *subject* that you know well and understand,

You will find it easier to write if you have ——— a clear *purpose* for writing,

an *audience* that you have identified.

Keeping these three elements in mind will help your writing stay focused.

Subject

In order to write well, it is helpful to choose a topic that interests you and that you know and understand. If you are assigned a subject, try to find an angle of that subject that you find interesting and want to explore. You will usually have to go through a process of narrowing down the general subject until you find an appropriate topic.

In the following example, the general subject *entertainment* has been narrowed down to *The 1993 Rolling Stones' World Tour.*

ENTERTAINMENT
Concerts
ROCK CONCERTS

Rolling Stones

'93 World Tour

In the next example, the same general subject, *entertainment*, has been narrowed down to the *silent film era*.

ENTERTAINMENT
The Movies
MOVIE HISTORY

Early History

Silent Film Era

FINDING A SUBJECT

Go through the process of narrowing down each of the following general subjects until you find a specific angle that you would be interested in writing about.

TELEVISION PROGRAMS

_____

_____

_____

_____

INNER-CITY CRIME

_____

_____

_____

_____

Write a few narrowed topics on the chalkboard. Different students will probably have very different topics. Discuss and compare the various topics with your classmates.

Purpose

Whenever you write something, it is important to think about your purpose. To determine your purpose, you should ask yourself the question "Why am I writing?" The three most common purposes for writing are **to entertain, to inform,** and **to persuade.** However, these three purposes are not always mutually exclusive. It is possible for a piece of writing to accomplish several purposes at the same time. An article, for example, may be amusing but also educational and/or persuasive.

IDENTIFYING PURPOSE

A. Read each of the following selections and decide whether the author's purpose is to entertain, to inform, or to persuade, or if it is a combination. Write your answer on the line.

Selection 1 _____

El Niño is the name given to an unusual warming of the Pacific Ocean that can cause weather changes all over the world. El Niño has plagued much of the world with disruptive weather for several years now, but researchers at the National Oceanic and Atmospheric Administration announced yesterday that El Niño's strength has dissipated. Long-range climate forecasts on events like El Niño can help farmers successfully choose which crops to plant. Forecasts in Peru, for example, have helped increase the nation's overall economic product by preventing millions of dollars' worth of crop losses.

Selection 2 _____

William Bennett, the former U.S. Secretary of Education, is focusing his attention and that of the nation on daytime TV talk shows. The objects of his scorn are those shows that bring on an endless parade of perverts, prostitutes, promiscuous spouses, and pornography stars, who contribute to our nation's cultural pollution. The shows are disgusting to watch and they are not what our young people should be tuning in to. These depraved shows have no socially redeeming qualities, except that they draw high ratings for their advertisers.

Selection 3 _____

There was a faith healer named Deal

Who said, "Although pain isn't real,

If I sit on a pin, and I puncture my skin

I dislike what I think that I feel!"

(author unknown)

(continued on next page)

Selection 4 _____

The president is due in Boston on February 13 for a campaign fund-raising dinner, the White House said yesterday. The president is expected to arrive in Boston aboard his private plane, *Air Force One,* after giving a speech at the Department of Health and Human Services in Washington, D. C. He will return to the White House later that night.

Selection 5 _____

It has been said that there is no love more sincere than the love of good food. You will surely agree when you join us for dinner at **The Atelier** in the heart of Soho.

Our highly acclaimed chef will attend to your every whim and fancy as you choose from our impressive menu of fine French cuisine, artfully prepared, presented, and served in our tastefully decorated restaurant.

Whether you're in New York for a special occasion or not, we'll make this occasion special. You'll fall in love.

Selection 6 _____

"Renting a car offers many attractive advantages to the traveler: independence, convenience, dependability, and a sudden, massive lowering of the IQ. I know what I'm talking about here. I live in Miami, and every winter we have a huge infestation of rental-car drivers, who come down here seeking warm weather and the opportunity to make sudden left turns without signaling, across six lanes of traffic, into convenience stores. My wife and I have affectionately nicknamed these people "Alamos," because so many of them seem to get their cars from Alamo, which evidently requires that every driver leave several major brain lobes as a deposit . . . We're tempted to stay off the highways altogether during tourist season, just stockpile food and spend the entire winter huddled in our bedrooms, but we're not sure we'd be safe *there.*"

Source: *Dave Barry's Only Travel Guide You'll Ever Need,* by Dave Barry

B. Complete the chart below by putting each type of writing in the appropriate box. Some types of writing may go in more than one box.

plays	jokes	newspaper articles
memos	stories	novels
songs	comparisons	letters
essays	editorials	textbooks
poetry	analyses	instructions

Entertain	Inform	Persuade

C. Look through your local newspaper and find one example of writing that entertains, one that informs, and one that persuades. Bring your articles to class to share with your classmates.

1. Which kind of article (entertaining, informational, or persuasive) was the easiest to find?

   _____

2. Which kind was the most difficult to find? Why?

   _____

3. Which kind of writing do you think students are usually asked to do?

   _____

✓Audience

What you write about (subject) and your reason for writing (purpose) are greatly affected by whom you expect will read the final product (audience). Because you will almost always be writing for an audience, you will communicate your ideas more effectively if you keep that audience in mind. Remember that all audiences have expectations, but those expectations vary from one audience to another.

As you work through this book, your audience will usually be your teacher or classmates. However, you will occasionally be asked to write with another audience in mind. This will give you practice in choosing the appropriate words and varying the tone of your writing.

Read the following two letters and notice the difference in tone.

Dear Sis,

Just a short note to let you know I'll be in Phoenix on the 8th for a business meeting. I'll have some free time that afternoon. Let's have lunch together. Let me know if this works for you. By the way, I bumped into your old friend Sally last week. She asked me how you were doing. I guess she hasn't heard from you in a while. Why don't you give her a call? See you soon.

Love,
Jack

Sunshine Industries
27 Laredo Drive
San Antonio, Texas 78250

September 21, 1998

John Hill, President
Indigo, Inc.
3140 East 10th Street
Phoenix, Arizona 85715

Dear Mr. Hill:

I am writing to let you know that I will be in Phoenix on October 8th and would like very much to meet with you and show you our new product line. If this is agreeable to you, I can meet you at your office at 4:00 P.M. I would be pleased if you would join me for dinner after our meeting. I look forward to hearing from you.

Sincerely,

Jack Norris

Jack Norris
Vice President of Sales

In small groups, make a list of the differences between the two letters. Which letter uses a more formal style?

1. _____
2. _____
3. _____
4. _____
5. _____

WRITING FOR DIFFERENT AUDIENCES

A letter you would write to your best friend asking him or her to lend you some money would be quite different from a letter to a bank loan officer. The two letters would probably include different expressions and have a different tone.

A. On a separate piece of paper, write a letter to your best friend asking to borrow money.

B. Then write a letter to the loan officer at a bank asking to borrow money.

C. Compare your two letters and answer the following questions:
   1. Which letter was easier for you to write? Why?
   2. In which letter did you use a more formal style?

Determining Subject, Purpose, and Audience

Choose one of the following general subjects to write a paragraph about:

- your hometown
- your school
- your family

After you have chosen your subject, find an angle of it that you find interesting. Then determine your purpose and identify your audience.

Subject: _____

Purpose: _____

Audience: _____

Finally, write your paragraph.

_____

_____

_____

_____

_____

_____

_____

_____

_____

_____

_____

Now find another angle of the same subject that you want to explore. Choose a different purpose for your writing and pick another audience.

Subject: _____

Purpose: _____

Audience: _____

Write a second paragraph.

_____

_____

_____

_____

_____

(continued on next page)

How are your two paragraphs alike? How are they different?

The Writing Process

Very few people pick up a pen or sit down at a computer and produce a perfect piece of writing on the first try. Most writers spend a lot of time thinking before they write and then work through a series of steps while they are composing. The final product is often the result of several careful revisions. It takes patience as well as skill to write well. You should think of writing as a process involving the following steps:

Step One: Prewriting
thinking about your topic

Step Two: Planning
organizing your material

Step Three: Drafting
using your ideas and plans to write a first draft

Step Four: Revising
improving the focus, content, and organization

Step Five: Editing
checking grammar, spelling, capitalization, punctuation, and word choices

Step One: Prewriting

Whether you enjoy writing or not, you will find it easier to write if you do some prewriting exercises to get started. For many people, the hardest part of writing is *getting started*. Following are several prewriting techniques that writers use to generate ideas. Although some of the techniques are more structured than others, you will see that they can all help you figure out what you want to say.

Method 1: Brainstorming

Brainstorming is a method used to generate a variety of ideas on a subject rapidly and spontaneously. It can be done alone or in a group. The purpose is to get down on paper as many ideas as possible without worrying about how you will use them. To brainstorm, you simply make a list of as many ideas as you can about a topic. Your list can include words, phrases, sentences, or even questions.

To brainstorm, follow these steps:

1. Begin with a broad topic.
2. Write down as many associations as you can in 10 minutes.
3. Add more items to your list by answering the questions *what, how, when, where, why,* and *who.*
4. Group the items on the list that go together.
5. Cross out items that do not belong.

Your list may seem very unfocused as you are working on it. But you will later go back and organize the items on your list and decide which ones you want to include in your essay and which you want to discard.

The following is an example of brainstorming on the general subject of *superstitions.*

Topic: Superstitions

Friday 13th

breaking a mirror

always wear pearl necklace for tests

look for four-leaf clovers

sit on left side of plane

sit in center of room for tests

wear lucky T-shirt for games

finding a penny

eat scrambled eggs for breakfast on day of a game

don't walk under ladders

don't step on cracks

wear green when I fly

use lucky shoelaces in tennis shoes

switch watch to right wrist for tests

never start a trip on Friday

In this example, after the author made her list, she read it over and decided to write an essay that focused on her personal superstitions. She grouped together similar ideas and eliminated items that did not fit in. In the end, she grouped her list into three categories: *superstitions about school, travel,* and *sports.*

School:

always wear pearl necklace for tests

sit in center of room for tests

switch watch to right wrist for tests

Travel:

sit on left side of plane

never start a trip on Friday

wear green when I fly

Sports:

wear lucky T-shirt for games

use lucky shoelaces in tennis shoes

eat scrambled eggs for breakfast on day of a game

BRAINSTORMING ACTIVITY

In the space below, brainstorm ideas for the general topic of *travel*.

Now, group similar ideas together and eliminate ones that do not fit in.

Method 2: Clustering

Clustering is a visual way of generating ideas. When using the clustering technique, you show the connections among your ideas using circles and lines. To cluster, follow these steps:

1. Write your topic in the center of a blank page and draw a circle around it.
2. Think about your topic and write any ideas that come to mind in circles around the main circle.
3. Connect these ideas to the center word with a line.
4. Think about each of your new ideas and write more related ideas in circles around them.
5. Connect your new circles to their corresponding ideas.
6. When you are finished, your most promising topic will probably be the one with the most circles connected to it.

On the next page is an example of a cluster diagram on the topic of *cars*. In this example, what topic or topics would the author probably choose to write about? Why?

_____

_____

_____

_____

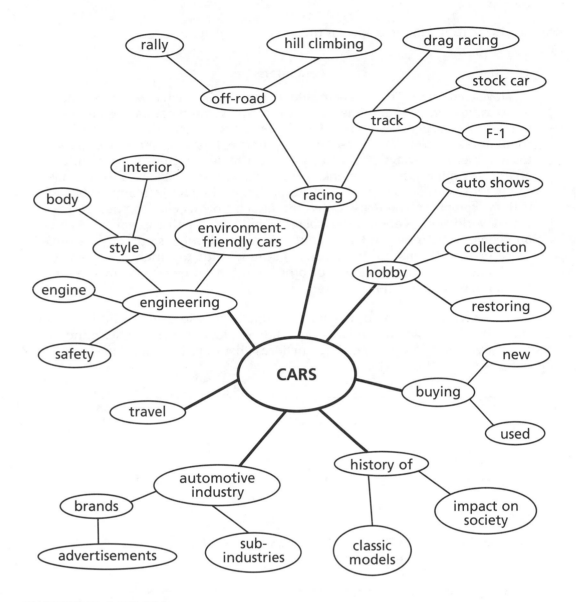

CLUSTERING ACTIVITY

On a separate piece of paper, practice clustering for an essay on the topic of *music*.

Method 3: Freewriting

Sometimes it is hard to find a focus for a broad subject. If this is your problem, freewriting can be very helpful. To freewrite, follow these steps:

1. Write your topic at the top of your page.
2. Start writing.
3. Write as much as you can and as fast as you can for 10 minutes.
4. Don't stop for any reason. Don't worry if your mind wanders away from your original idea; let your ideas flow.
5. If you can't think of anything, write "my mind is blank, my mind is blank," or something similar, over and over again until a new thought comes into your mind.
6. Don't worry about mistakes. Just keep writing. You can go back later and edit.
7. Read your freewriting and see if there are any ideas you can develop into a paragraph.

Read the freewriting sample below on the topic of *computers*.

Computers

I love computers. They make my life so much easier than it was when I had to use a typewriter every time I wanted to type something. Back then I had to start all over again whenever I made a mistake. I really don't understand computers very well. Whenever I have a problem, I have to get someone else to help me. I'm always afraid to try to fix it myself. I guess I'm computer-phobic. My mind just went blank. It went blank. It went blank. Just like my computer screen does when I have a problem. And I have so many problems with my computer. There are always technical problems with computers. The whole world worries about technical problems. They are so unpredictable and unreliable. What else can I say about computers? I only use them for word processing and e-mail. I enjoy communicating with my friends by e-mail. That's all. I know there are lots of other uses but I'll never get involved in them. I don't understand computers.

When you freewrite, your mind may jump around as new ideas come into it. You can see that as this author was writing, new and different ideas came into her mind. In the example above, there are several different ideas that could be developed into paragraphs. List some of them below.

_____

_____

_____

Compare your list with a classmate's. Did you include the same items?

FREEWRITING ACTIVITY

Write for 10 minutes on the subject of *your plans for the future.* Your teacher will tell you when to begin and when to stop writing.

_____

_____

_____

_____

_____

_____

_____

_____

_____

_____

_____

Did you generate any ideas that you could now write a paragraph about? If so, what are they?

_____

_____

_____

Method 4: Keeping a Journal

Journal writing is a technique that is popular with many writers. When you are not given a specific subject to write on, you can refer to your journal for possible topics. If you decide to keep a journal, start by buying a notebook and writing in it for a few minutes every day. Use the time to write about anything you want. For example, you could write about the events of your day, the people you met or talked to, or your reaction to something that you heard, read, or saw.

Use your journal as a record of your daily thoughts and activities, as a means of self-expression, or as a way of understanding yourself better. No matter what your original reason for keeping a journal, you will find it a valuable source of material in your future writing and thinking.

Here is an example of a journal entry:

November 19

I just got back from an ice hockey game. Ray had an extra ticket and asked me if I wanted it. The Boston Bruins beat the St. Louis Blues 5-2. Our seats were really high up, almost to the roof, but we could still see more than if we had watched it on television. It's so much easier to see the puck when you are there than when you watch a game on TV. I started talking to the old man sitting next to me about hockey in "the good old days." He went to his first hockey game in 1939—the game when the Bruins won the second Stanley Cup World Championship in a row! He talked on and on about the changes he has seen in the kinds of equipment, rules, and the style of play since his day. He remembers when players weren't required to wear helmets, but he said that the play was less rough back then. There weren't as many fights. I wonder if that's really true. Hockey has always been a pretty physical game, and I bet emotions have always run high among the players. It was a good game. I hope Ray can get me tickets to more games this season. It looks like the Bruins might be good this year.

List several of the general topics from this journal entry that the author might use to develop a paragraph.

_____

_____

_____

Compare your list with a classmate's. Did you include the same items?

JOURNAL-WRITING ACTIVITY

Use the journal page below to write your first journal entry. Write about something that happened to you recently.

Step Two: Planning

The purpose of prewriting is to generate ideas for writing. The next step is to do some planning. At this stage of the writing process, your main goal is to organize your ideas. Preparing an informal outline of the ideas you generated from prewriting will help you organize your thoughts as you plan your paragraph. You can use your outline as a guide that you refer to while you are composing.

Here is an example of an informal outline based on the ideas generated from brainstorming on the topic *superstitions*. Notice that the three headings in this outline are the same three categories determined in the brainstorming exercise.

Topic: My Superstitions

1. Superstitions about school
   a. always wear pearl necklace for tests
   b. sit in center of room for tests
   c. switch watch to right wrist for tests

2. Superstitions about travel
   a. sit on left side of plane
   b. never start a trip on Friday
   c. wear green when I fly

3. Superstitions about sports
   a. wear lucky T-shirt for games
   b. use lucky shoelaces in tennis shoes
   c. eat scrambled eggs for breakfast on day of a game

INFORMAL OUTLINING ACTIVITY

1. Prepare an informal outline based on the groups of similar ideas you created in the brainstorming exercise about *travel* on page 12.

   TOPIC: TRAVEL

2. Prepare an informal outline based on your clustering diagram on *music* on page 13.

   TOPIC: MUSIC

Chapter Highlights

1. How is writing like driving a car? What other skill can you compare writing to?

_____

_____

_____

2. List and explain the three things you should consider when you write something.

_____

_____

_____

3. What are the five basic steps in the writing process?

_____

_____

_____

_____

_____

4. What are the four common prewriting techniques you learned about in this chapter?

_____

_____

_____

_____

Drafting Paragraphs

After you have spent some time thinking about your topic and doing the necessary prewriting and planning, you are ready for the next step in the writing process: drafting.

Step Three: Drafting

As you write your first draft, use as a guide the ideas you generated from prewriting and the organizational plan you developed in your informal outline. In this step of the writing process, you should be concerned with two things: **stating your point** and **supporting your point**. Do not worry about producing a perfect paragraph on the first draft.

Here is an example of a paragraph drafted from the informal outline on *superstitions* on page 17. Remember that this is only a first draft, so it is not perfect.

I am a very superstitious person. First of all, I have a lot of superstitions about school, especially tests. For example, I always wear the pearl necklace that my grandmother gave me when I have to take a test. I think it brings me good luck, and I am afraid that I will do poorly if I forget to wear it. When I get to school, I always find a seat right in the middle of the room, sit down, and then switch my watch to my right wrist before the test begins. In addition, I am very superstitious about traveling. I will never start a trip on a Friday because I am sure it will bring me bad luck. When I'm flying somewhere, I make sure to get a seat on the left side of the plane and always wear something green, my lucky color. Finally, like many other athletes, I am especially superstitious when it comes to my sport, tennis. When I dress for a match, I always wear the same white T-shirt with my initials on it. I also use the same shoelaces in my sneakers that I've had since I first started playing tennis. As soon as I buy a new pair of sneakers, the first thing I do is replace the laces with my lucky ones. I am also superstitious about my breakfast on the day of a match. I always eat the same thing: two scrambled eggs and a blueberry muffin.

Notice that this and all paragraphs contain the following important features:

a. The first sentence is indented.
b. The first word of every sentence is capitalized.
c. Each sentence ends with a period.

Stating Your Point

When you write a paragraph in English, the most important thing you need to do is to decide on your main point. This should be written in one clear sentence, called the **topic sentence**. The rest of the paragraph must develop and support the point you made in the topic sentence.

Analyzing Paragraphs

Read the next two paragraphs and answer the questions that follow.

Paragraph 1

The English language has some truly remarkable statistics. Out of the world's 6,000 languages, English has the richest vocabulary, with over 500,000 words and an additional half million scientific and technical terms. It is the native language of over 400 million people scattered across every continent. In fact, English is used in some way by one out of seven human beings around the globe, making it the most widely spoken language in history. There are also some astonishing facts about written English. Approximately 50 percent of the world's books are published in English. In addition, three-quarters of all mail, faxes, and cables are written in English. Similarly, more than half of all scientific and technical journals are written in English, making it truly the international language of technology. Over 90 percent of all the information stored in computers around the world is in English. Technology is not the only area where English is the dominant language. Over half of all business deals in Europe are conducted in English and many more are negotiated in English in other parts of the international business community. English is also the language of sports and glamor. It is the official language of both the Olympics and the Miss Universe Pageant. Finally, English is the language of over 60 percent of the world's radio and TV programs. Most of the large broadcasting companies transmit their programs in English all over the world.

Paragraph 2

The English language has been around for a long time, and more and more people are learning to speak it. It is the official language of the Olympics and even the Miss Universe Pageant, which people around the world like to watch. Last year the winner was from Norway. Business deals and scientific research are also done in English. Most technical journals are written in English, so it is a good idea to learn English if you are planning to go into any of these fields. Some students find English quite difficult to master because of the large vocabulary and difficult pronunciation. I have been studying this language for several years and still have trouble with some of the complicated grammar rules. If you enjoy watching TV or listening to the radio, you must realize that many programs are broadcast in English. Lots of great movies have also been made in English, so if you know how to speak it, you won't have to worry about reading the subtitles. However, I really enjoy films from all around the world. Some of my favorite movies were made in France and Italy. Since one out of seven people worldwide uses English in one way or another, it will probably continue to be an important language in the future. And if you like to read, you should know that about half of the world's books are published in English.

1. Which paragraph do you think is clearer?

     _____

2. What is the main point of that paragraph?

     _____

     _____

3. Is that point stated in a clearly written topic sentence?

     _____

4. What do you think are the problems with the other paragraph?

_____

_____

_____

Topic Sentences

The topic sentence is usually the first sentence of a paragraph. It is the most important one in your paragraph because it controls all the other sentences. In this way, a topic sentence functions like a traffic sign controlling vehicles on the road. It shows readers which way they are going, just as a traffic sign helps direct drivers.

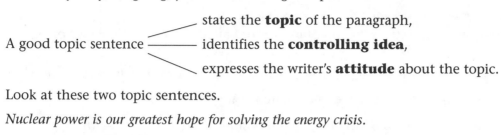

A good topic sentence
— states the **topic** of the paragraph,
— identifies the **controlling idea**,
— expresses the writer's **attitude** about the topic.

Look at these two topic sentences.

Nuclear power is our greatest hope for solving the energy crisis.

1. What is the topic of this sentence?

_____

2. What is the controlling idea?

_____

Nuclear power is the greatest threat to life on the planet.

1. What is the topic of this sentence?

_____

2. What is the controlling idea?

_____

Notice that both sentences have the same topic, but the controlling ideas are different.

Analyzing Topic Sentences

For each statement below, underline the topic and draw a circle around the controlling idea.

1. Martin Luther King Jr. was an influential leader.
2. The editorials in our school newspaper are not very objective.
3. The clothes we wear often reflect a lot about our personality.
4. The Japanese subway system is very efficient.
5. Television commercials are often insulting to women.
6. My older brother is a perfectionist.
7. The laws on child abuse should be strictly enforced.
8. Being a twin has both advantages and disadvantages.
9. The new shopping mall has brought many economic benefits to our community.
10. Golf is a difficult sport to master.

There are several common mistakes students make when writing topic sentences. You should avoid these three mistakes:

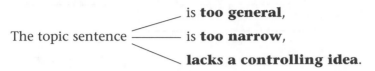

The topic sentence — is **too general**,
— is **too narrow**,
— **lacks a controlling idea**.

Read the following topic sentences about *exercise* that illustrate these mistakes:

1. *Many people like to exercise.*
This statement is too broad to be developed adequately into one paragraph.

2. *I swim laps for 30 minutes every morning.*
This statement is too narrow to be developed into a paragraph.

3. *The subject of this paragraph is my exercise routine.*
This statement simply states the topic but does not identify a controlling idea or express the writer's attitude.

If you can avoid making these mistakes, the rest of the paragraph will be easier to write.

Here is an example of an effective topic sentence about *exercise:*

> *Exercising every morning has several positive effects on my health.*

This statement contains a clear topic and controlling idea that could be developed into one paragraph.

Evaluating Topic Sentences

Read the following statements and put a checkmark next to the three that you think are effective topic sentences. Then figure out why each of the other sentences is not effective. Is it too general? Too narrow? Does it lack a controlling idea? Draw a line through those sentences and rewrite them.

_____ 1. Vacations are expensive.

_____ 2. My round-trip plane ticket to Orlando, Florida, cost over $550.

_____ 3. There are several ways to save money on a vacation to Disney World and still have a good time.

_____ 4. I am going to write about the trip I took to Disney World last summer.

_____ 5. American music reflects the native music of many of its immigrant groups.

_____ 6. I love music.

_____ 7. The history of American music is the subject of this paper.

_____ 8. The first published collection of Afro-American music, *Slave Songs of the United States*, appeared in 1867.

_____ 9. Russian is a difficult language to learn.

_____ 10. Learning how to write in a foreign language can be a frustrating experience for many students.

_____ 11. There are over 50,000 characters in the Chinese language.

_____ 12. The topic of this essay is learning to write in a foreign language.

Writing Topic Sentences

Write a topic sentence for each of the paragraphs below. Be sure that each one states the main point and expresses a controlling idea.

EXAMPLE:

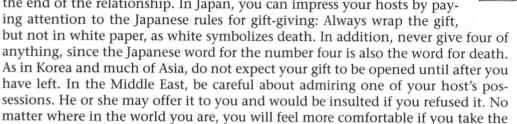

The customs associated with giving gifts vary from country to country.

Whether you are a tourist, a student, or a businessperson, it is important to know the gift-giving customs of the country you are visiting. For example, if you are invited for dinner, flowers are a safe and appreciated gift throughout the world. In some places, however, you must take care not to offend. In much of Europe, red roses symbolize romance and would be inappropriate. In Austria and Germany, it is considered bad luck to receive an even number of flowers. If you are in Hong Kong, gifts to avoid are clocks, which symbolize death, and scissors or knives, which indicate the end of the relationship. In Japan, you can impress your hosts by paying attention to the Japanese rules for gift-giving: Always wrap the gift, but not in white paper, as white symbolizes death. In addition, never give four of anything, since the Japanese word for the number four is also the word for death. As in Korea and much of Asia, do not expect your gift to be opened until after you have left. In the Middle East, be careful about admiring one of your host's possessions. He or she may offer it to you and would be insulted if you refused it. No matter where in the world you are, you will feel more comfortable if you take the time to learn some of the local gift-giving customs.

Source: *Dos and Taboos Around the World*

1. _____

Most importantly, they are kept for pleasure and companionship. In fact, many people consider their pet to be part of the family. In addition to their value as loved and loving companions, pets serve practical purposes, such as protecting homes and property, destroying vermin, and even providing means of transportation. They may also serve as emotional outlets for the elderly or the childless. Recently, the benefit of pet-facilitated psychotherapy has been demonstrated. Finally, some people keep pets for their beauty or rarity or, in the case of birds, for their songs.

Source: *Encarta*, 1994

2. _____

For instance, climate affects the kinds of clothes we wear and even the colors we choose to wear. Since it affects the kinds of crops we can grow successfully, it influences our eating habits. Architecture is also affected by climate. Engineers and architects must think about climate when they make decisions about the construction, materials, design, and style of buildings. Even our choices in transportation are determined by the climate in which we live. Climate also plays a big part in economic development. A climate that is too hot, too cold, or too dry makes farming, industry, and transportation difficult and slows down economic development.

(continued on next page)

3. _____

Symptoms may last for one day or several days and vary greatly in severity. Chronobiologists, scientists who study the effects of time on living things, say that the seriousness of your reaction depends on several factors. One factor is the number of time zones you crossed. Your jet lag will probably be worse if you crossed several time zones. Another factor is whether you flew east to west or west to east. It is easier to adjust after an east-to-west flight. Personality factors also affect how easily you adapt to the new time. For example, "night" people adapt more easily than "morning" people. Extroverts adjust more easily than introverts. Flexible people who don't mind changes have fewer problems than inflexible people who are rigid and don't like change. Younger people suffer less than older people. Finally, healthier people usually get over jet lag more easily than people who are sick.

4. _____

For example, True Value hardware stores sold half a million shovels during the winter of 1994. This was up 75 percent from the year before. Customers also bought 50 million pounds of rock salt, which is used to melt ice. Ice scrapers were another "hot" item. ServiStar's sales of ice scrapers in December, January, and February equaled sales of the past four years combined. Finally, sales of winter clothes were higher than ever. For example, hat sales were up 13 percent, and retailers sold about 95 million pairs of gloves. One company, L. L. Bean, usually sells 150,000 pairs of its most popular winter boot, but during the winter of '94, it sold over 350,000 pairs.

Write several topic sentences on the chalkboard to compare and discuss.

Supporting Your Point

After you have stated your point in a clearly written topic sentence, you will need to support it by giving the reader reasons, facts, and examples.

Look back at Paragraph 1 on page 20 and make a list of the supporting details the author used to develop the main idea.

a. _____

b. _____

c. _____

d. _____

e. _____

f. _____

Analyzing Paragraphs for Support

A paragraph that does not have enough support is considered underdeveloped. As a writer, it is your job to provide enough support to prove the point you made in your topic sentence. Your supporting sentences should be as specific as possible. Supporting sentences that are vague or that merely repeat the point you made in the topic sentence are not effective.

Look at the following two paragraphs. Both begin with the topic sentence *Our family trip to Costa Rica last summer was very exciting,* but only one develops it with specific support. Choose the paragraph that you think provides enough specific support.

Paragraph 1

Our family trip to Costa Rica last summer was very exciting. Every day we saw something new and different. One day we went hiking, which was really an incredible experience. Another day we took a rafting trip down a river. We saw lots of unusual plants and animals that we had never seen before. We did many things that we will never forget. Everyone agreed that this was the best trip we have ever taken.

Paragraph 2

Our family trip to Costa Rica last summer was very exciting. We were there for two weeks, and not a day went by without something unusual happening. On our second day, a boa constrictor swam right in front of us while we were rafting down the Río Claro. Another day, spider monkeys threw branches at us deep in the rain forest. Hiking on the primitive trails in Corcovado National Park, we saw brilliant scarlet macaws and toucans with huge yellow beaks. Whenever we look at the pictures from our trip, we all agree that it was the most exciting one we've ever taken.

Evaluating Support

Read the following sets of paragraphs and answer the questions. Each paragraph begins with a clear topic sentence, but only one paragraph in each set develops the main point with adequate support.

A.

Paragraph 1

The repairs on my car were much more expensive than I had anticipated. When I saw the final bill, I was in shock. It was twice as much as I had planned on. I had to pay $395 to get the brakes repaired and another $100 to get the wheels aligned. The engine oil change was $30, and the replacement of the air filter was another $20.

Paragraph 2

The repairs on my car were much more expensive than I had anticipated. The mechanic did a good job, but I think I was overcharged for everything. I never imagined that the final bill would be so high. In fact, I had to borrow some money from my friend to pay it. The next time my car needs repairs, I'll go to a different garage.

1. Which paragraph provides more specific support?

   _____

2. What four supporting details does the author include in that paragraph?

   _____

   _____

   _____

   _____

(continued on next page)

B.

Paragraph 1

My chemistry course is very difficult and time-consuming. The professor doesn't seem to realize that chemistry isn't the only course we are taking. He gives lots of homework and too much reading. The material is very hard and his tests and quizzes are impossible. All the students are complaining about this course.

Paragraph 2

My chemistry course is very difficult and time-consuming. We are responsible for two labs every week, which means a minimum of ten hours a week in the lab. The professor gives at least three tests per month. The questions are very tricky, and we have to memorize long, complicated formulas. The reading load is also quite heavy—as much as twenty-five pages a night. I often spend all my free time doing the required reading.

1. Which paragraph provides more specific support?

     _____

2. What four supporting details does the author include in the paragraph?

     _____

     _____

     _____

     _____

C.

Paragraph 1

My apartment is in a terrible location. First of all, it is too far away from the important stores and services. It is several miles from a grocery store, and I have to take two buses to get there. There are no local banks, laundromats, hardware stores, or pharmacies that I can walk to from my apartment. My apartment is also in a high-crime area. Gangs of teenagers roam the streets, threatening the neighbors. Last month alone there were eight robberies on our block. The elderly woman who lives next door had her purse snatched while she was walking her dog. In addition, because my apartment is near an industrial area, the pollution is awful. There is so much smog from the chemical plant that it is often hard for me to breathe. Finally, there is no convenient public transportation in my neighborhood. The one bus line near my apartment runs only one bus an hour and has a very limited route. Almost everywhere I need to go involves changing buses and takes a lot of time.

Paragraph 2

My apartment is in a horrible place. I wish I didn't live in this neighborhood, but I can't afford to move. I've lived here for years and the rent is reasonable. I guess you get what you pay for. There is nothing close by and I have to waste a lot of time getting anywhere I want to go. If the location were more convenient, I wouldn't mind living here so much. To make matters worse, I am always afraid to go out alone after dark and am constantly looking over my shoulder when I do. No one wants to visit me because they think it's too dangerous around here. I also hate the fact that I'm so close to a chemical plant. I'd rather be near a mall where I could go shopping. There is nothing interesting to do around here. My neighbors are very boring and don't seem to mind living in this terrible neighborhood. Most of my friends have moved to nicer areas because of all the problems I've mentioned.

1. Which paragraph provides more specific support?

     _____

2. What four main supporting points does the author include in the paragraph?

_____

_____

_____

_____

D.

Paragraph 1

The effects of global warming on the environment could be disastrous. For one thing, deserts will become hotter and drier and continue to expand. Rising seas, caused in part by the melting of half the world's mountain glaciers, will flood low-lying islands and coasts, threatening millions of people. Global warming will change the climate regionally and globally, altering natural vegetation and affecting crop production. Indeed, all kinds of plants and forests, from the tropics to the Arctic tundra, will undergo radical transformation. Finally, higher temperatures could also cause more extreme storms, allowing tropical diseases to invade temperate areas.

Paragraph 2

A warming of the atmosphere would have serious environmental effects. Something needs to be done about this. Once it begins, the trend toward warmer temperatures could be irreversible. It would speed up the melting of ice caps and raise sea levels. An increase in atmospheric carbon dioxide of 10 percent over the past century has led some authorities to predict a long-term warming of the Earth's climate. This warming could have a severe impact on our environment and the world as we know it. Over 150 nations have signed a 1992 treaty to reduce the emission of gases that intensify the greenhouse effect and result in global warming. Since global warming would probably have a negative effect on our environment, I hope all nations take the treaty seriously.

1. Which paragraph is vague, repetitive, and lacks enough support to prove the point?

_____

2. Which sentences in that paragraph merely restate the topic?

_____

_____

_____

_____

3. Which sentences are true but do not really support the point that global warming could have a profound effect on the environment?

_____

_____

_____

_____

Practice Writing Supporting Sentences

Write three supporting sentences for each of the following topic sentences.

EXAMPLE:

I am terrible at doing the laundry.

a. *I often shrink my favorite shirts because I leave them in the dryer for too long.*

b. *I forget to separate the colored clothes from the white ones and sometimes end up with gray underwear.*

c. *I rarely read the cleaning instructions and have ruined things that should have been dry-cleaned by putting them in the washing machine.*

1. I love eating food from different countries.

   a. _____

   b. _____

   c. _____

2. Summer is my favorite season.

   a. _____

   b. _____

   c. _____

3. There is a lot of violence on television.

   a. _____

   b. _____

   c. _____

4. There are several ways to conserve electricity.

   a. _____

   b. _____

   c. _____

5. It is almost impossible to study in my dormitory.

   a. _____

   b. _____

   c. _____

Choose the topic sentence that you have the best support for and develop it into a paragraph.

_____

_____

_____

_____

_____

_____

_____

_____

_____

_____

_____

Exchange paragraphs with a classmate. Check to make sure that your partner's topic sentence has enough support.

Supplying Specific Details

To write a fully developed paragraph, you will often need to provide specific details to strengthen your main supporting points. The following paragraphs each have a topic sentence and three or four main supporting points. With a classmate, complete the paragraphs by adding your own specific details to clarify each supporting point.

1. My mother nags me constantly. For one thing, my room is never clean enough to suit her. _Although I hang up my clothes at least once a week, she expects me to put them away every night before I go to bed. She also hates it if I leave any food, wrappers, or soda cans in my room._ In addition, she never thinks I've spent enough time on my schoolwork. _____

_____

_____

_____

Finally, she is always bugging me about my appearance. _____

_____

_____

_____

(continued on next page)

2. After my grandfather moved in with us, I began to realize the benefits of living with an older person. First of all, he has told me a lot of stories about our family history. _____

_____

_____

_____

Since my grandfather is retired, he has been able to spend a lot of time helping me with my schoolwork. _____

_____

_____

_____

Most importantly, I've learned to appreciate the special qualities an older person can have. _____

_____

_____

_____

3. There are many ways to economize on a trip to Europe and still have a good time. First, you can shop around for the best airfare. _____

_____

_____

_____

Once you get there, you do not need to stay in the most expensive five-star hotels.

_____

_____

_____

You can also economize on food. _____

_____

_____

_____

Finally, you should take advantage of all the free cultural and historical offerings.

_____

_____

_____

Drafting a Paragraph

1. Choose one of the topics below to develop into a paragraph.
   a. Benefits of having a job that requires a lot of travel
   b. Reasons you would or would not join an expedition to the South Pole
   c. Reasons that you chose your career or major
   d. Ways colors affect you
   e. Reasons you would or would not like to be a movie star
2. Use one of the prewriting techniques you practiced in Chapter 1 to get you started.
3. Organize the ideas you generated by preparing an informal outline.
4. Write a topic sentence for your paragraph that contains a controlling idea.

---

5. On a separate piece of paper, draft the paragraph. Remember to develop each of your supporting points with specific details. Introduce your main points with *first of all*, *in addition*, and *finally* to help guide your reader from one idea to the next.

Unity

In addition to a clear topic sentence and adequate support, a good paragraph must have **unity**. A paragraph is unified when all of the supporting sentences relate to the main topic and develop the controlling idea. In order to achieve unity, you must make sure that you do not include any information that is not relevant to the main point stated in the topic sentence. Any sentences that do not support the topic are considered irrelevant and should be eliminated.

Practicing Unity

A. The topic of the following paragraph is Boston's annual New Year's Eve celebration. As you read it, decide which sentences do not belong in the paragraph because they do not support the topic. Cross out the irrelevant sentences.

Boston was the first city in the United States to launch a special event to celebrate New Year's Eve. Called First Night, the Boston New Year's celebration is now an annual event that attracts over 1.5 million people. Boston is the higher-education capital of America. The two largest universities within the city itself are Boston University and Northeastern University. In nearby Cambridge are Harvard University and Massachusetts Institute of Technology. The evening begins with a grand costumed parade around the Boston Common and ends at midnight with fireworks over Boston Harbor. In between, there are more than 200 performances of international music, dance, and theater, as well as puppetry and many films to choose from. Boston is also host to the well-known Boston Marathon, which is run in April. For the $8.00

Photo © Kindra Clineff MCMXCII

(continued on next page)

cost of a First Night button, people gain general admission to the events. The purpose of First Night is to create good will and promote anticipation of a happy new year. Ninety cities in the United States, Canada, and Australia have now launched similar celebrations for New Year's Eve.

Which sentences did you cross out? Compare the ones you deleted with those your classmates deleted.

B. Now read the following paragraph and underline the topic sentence. Then decide if any of the sentences are irrelevant and cross them out.

If you are prone to mental or physical stress while flying, there are several precautions you can take to protect yourself. First of all, you might consider taking a Fearful Flier workshop. The purpose of this workshop is to help replace the myths about flying with facts, such as what makes a plane fly and how crews are trained. There are also many interesting workshops you can take to relieve stress at work. Planning ahead is a second way to cut down on stress. Leave plenty of time for your drive to the airport and have your travel agent make an advance seat assignment for you in a part of the plane you like. Many airports have shops and restaurants where you can spend time between flights. Third, communicate your fears. If the flight crew knows that a passenger is anxious, they will make more of an effort to put you at ease. Another tip is to stay loose, both physically and mentally. Wear loose, comfortable clothing and try to relax. Flex your hands and feet. Get up and walk around. Unfortunately, the food served on many flights is unappetizing. Fifth, don't allow yourself to get bored. Bring along a good book, some magazines, or a lot of absorbing work. Another precaution you can take is to drink plenty of water and fruit juices so that you don't become dehydrated from the pressurized cabin air. Dehydration is one of the most common causes of discomfort among air travelers. Last but not least, keep your ears open by swallowing, chewing gum, or talking.

Source: *Car and Travel, Nov.–Dec. 1995*

Which sentences did you cross out? Compare the ones you deleted with the ones your classmates deleted.

Coherence

By now you should realize that an effective paragraph needs a clear topic, adequate support, and unity. One more component of a good paragraph is **coherence.** In a coherent paragraph, the sentences are arranged so that the ideas are in a logical order. In order to achieve coherence, you need:

1. A clear plan of **arrangement**
2. **Transitions** to connect your ideas

1. Time order
2. spatial order
3. order of importance.

1. Arrangement

There are several standard ways to arrange your information so that your writing will be coherent. Three of the most basic ways are **time order, spatial order,** and **order of importance.**

The way you choose to arrange your information depends on the kind of paragraph you are writing. If you are explaining a sequence of events or telling a story, the logical arrangement of ideas and sentences will be chronological, that is, according to time order. If you are describing the way something looks or its physical characteristics, you will arrange your details according to the position of the objects being described or where they are located. In this case you will use spatial order. Finally, if you are listing examples, causes, effects, reasons, or purposes, you will probably use order of importance. In this type of paragraph, you either begin with the least important item and end with the most important one, or vice versa.

Analyzing Arrangement

Read the following three paragraphs. Determine the method of organization the author used in each paragraph: time order, spatial order, or order of importance.

A.

My anthropology teacher likes a classroom layout that encourages interaction among students. He sets up the physical space so that it encourages us to interact with each other as much as possible. He likes to have his desk in the center of the room. That means that the students surround him and everyone can always see everyone else. As you walk into the room, the first thing you see is the enormous windows directly opposite the door. If you look to the left, you will see his bulletin boards, which take up the entire back wall of the room. To the right is the computer station with enough computers for ten students. Behind you as you face the windows are the chalkboards. Above the boards, ready to be rolled down whenever we need them, are many different maps of the world. This type of classroom may not work for every teacher, but it works very well for Mr. Carter.

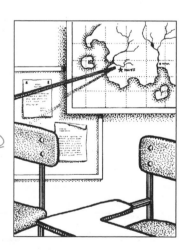

Method of arrangement: _____

B.

Behavioral scientists are interested in the complex navigational system of homing pigeons. Homing pigeons have been known to fly more than 1,600 kilometers in two days. According to the most recent research, homing pigeons use a combination of several navigational cues. One cue they use is the position of the sun. Using the sun as their compass, they compensate for its apparent movement, see both ultraviolet and polarized light, and employ a backup compass for cloudy days. Another navigational cue homing pigeons

(continued on next page)

use is based on their mental map of the landmarks in their home areas. Even if a pigeon is taken hundreds of kilometers from its loft in total darkness, it will depart almost directly for home when it is released. The most important cue homing pigeons use is the magnetic field of the earth. Their magnetic compass enables homing pigeons to navigate on cloudy and foggy days.

Method of arrangement: _____

C.

"Water covers almost three-quarters of the earth's surface. Over 97 percent of all this water is stored in the earth's four huge oceans: the Pacific, Atlantic, Indian, and Arctic Oceans. However, the earth has not always had oceans. Millions of years ago it was just a ball of hot rock. Its surface was covered with erupting volcanoes which released huge amounts of gas, including a gas made up of water particles, called water vapour. Eventually the Earth cooled, causing the water vapour to turn back into liquid water and fall from the skies as torrential rain. The rain lasted for thousands and thousands of years and gradually filled all the hollows around the earth's surface, forming oceans and seas."

Source: *The USBORNE Geography Encyclopedia*

Method of arrangement: _____

Practicing Arrangement

1. Think about the steps involved in planning a weekend trip to another city. Make a list of the steps and arrange them in time order.

   STEPS

   • _____

   • _____

   • _____

   • _____

   • _____

Write a paragraph based on your list and save your paper.

_____

_____

_____

_____

_____

_____

_____

_____

_____

_____

_____

_____

_____

2. What could someone learn about you from looking at your bedroom? Make a list of the items you want to describe and their placement in the room. Arrange your list according to spatial order.

ITEMS:

- _____
- _____
- _____
- _____
- _____
- _____
- _____

Using spatial order, write a paragraph describing how your bedroom reflects your personality.

_____

_____

_____

_____

_____

_____

_____

_____

_____

_____

_____

3. If you could live in any time period (past, present, or future), which one would you pick? Choose one and make a list of your reasons. Arrange the list in order of importance. You can begin or end with your most important reason.

REASONS

- _____
- _____
- _____

(continued on next page)

Write a paragraph based on your list.

_____

_____

_____

_____

_____

_____

_____

_____

_____

_____

_____

2. Transitions

Transitions are signals that show the connection between one idea and the next. They are important because they guide the reader through a paragraph. The following lists give some common transitions that will help make your paragraphs more coherent. You will learn more transitions as you work through this book.

Signals That Indicate Time Relationships		
first	then	next
earlier	later	eventually
before	after	as
while	meanwhile	since
soon afterward	from then on	at last
by the time		

Signals That Indicate Spatial Relationships		
to the left	beside	behind
to the right	across	at the center
in front of	above	between
in back of	below	near
next to		

Signals That Introduce Additional Ideas		
first of all	besides	finally
second	furthermore	last
the third reason	in addition	the most important
next	moreover	another reason
also		

Signals That Introduce an Illustration or Example		
for example	as an illustration	especially
for instance	to illustrate	such as
specifically		

Identifying Transitions

Look back at the three paragraphs on pages 33 and 34 and underline the transition signals.

1. What kind of transitions were used in the paragraph describing the classroom?

   _____

2. What kind of transitions did the author use to discuss the navigational cues of homing pigeons?

   _____

3. What kind of transitions were used to explain the formation of oceans?

   _____

Practice Using Transitions

Improve the three paragraphs you just wrote on pages 34–36 by adding transition signals to help guide your reader. Rewrite your paragraphs on a separate piece of paper.

Chapter Highlights

Complete the following paragraphs by filling in the blanks. You do not have to use exact words from the chapter as long as the ideas are correct.

The most important sentence in a paragraph is the _____.

This sentence _____ everything else that goes into your

paragraph. All the other sentences _____ by

_____. The topic sentence should state the

_____ and _____. In order to write

an effective topic sentence, you should avoid making the following mistakes:

(continued on next page)

_____, _____, and

_____.

You will always need to support your topic sentences with

_____. In addition to a clear topic sentence and adequate

support, a good paragraph must also have _____ and

_____. A paragraph is unified if all the supporting details

_____ to the main topic and _____

the controlling idea. In a coherent paragraph, the sentences are organized in a

_____. _____ are used to connect

one idea to the next.

Three of the most basic ways to organize information in a paragraph are by

_____, _____, and

_____.

On Your Own

Choose one of the following topics and write a paragraph. Be sure that your paragraph
has a clear topic sentence, adequate support, unity, and coherence.

1. Qualities of a good doctor
2. The layout of your favorite shop
3. Reasons you like (or do not like) modern art
4. Reasons cigarette advertising should (or should not) be banned
5. Ways to get good grades
6. How to make a copy of a computer disc
7. The layout of a baseball field, basketball court, hockey rink, or soccer field

Drafting Essays

Essay writing builds on many of the skills you have already mastered in learning to write a paragraph. Once you know how to write a paragraph, it is not much more difficult to write an essay; an essay is just longer. Simply stated, an essay is a set of paragraphs about a specific subject. Like a paragraph, an essay makes and supports one main point. However, the subject of an essay is too complex to be developed in a few sentences. To support fully the main point of an essay, several paragraphs are needed. A typical essay contains five paragraphs, but many other types of essays are longer or shorter, depending on their purpose. In this book, you will learn the formula for a five-paragraph essay. Just as knowing the musical scales will help you compose music, understanding basic essay structure will help you write well.

Although many essays do not conform to the five-paragraph formula, most follow some pattern of organization. The formula is simply a plan to help you arrange your ideas into a systematic order. It has a recognizable beginning, middle, and end. If you know how to write a typical five-paragraph essay, you will always have something to fall back on.

Parts of an Essay

An essay has three main parts: an **introduction,** a **body,** and a **conclusion.** Each part has its own special purpose. Briefly, the introduction provides some background information on the subject and states the main point in a thesis statement. The body consists of several supporting paragraphs that develop the main idea. The essay ends with a conclusion that summarizes the main points.

BASIC PLAN OF A TYPICAL FIVE-PARAGRAPH ESSAY

INTRODUCTION

INTRODUCTION

Background Information

Gets reader's attention using:

Facts and statistics

Quotations

Anecdotes

Questions

Thesis Statement

States purpose

Introduces 3 main points

(continued on next page)

FIRST BODY PARAGRAPH

Topic Sentence

    States first main point

    Provides supporting details

SECOND BODY PARAGRAPH

Topic Sentence

BODY   States second main point

    Provides supporting details

THIRD BODY PARAGRAPH

Topic Sentence

    States third main point

    Provides supporting details

CONCLUSION

    Makes final comments by:

    Summarizing main points

CONCLUSION   Drawing a conclusion

    Making a prediction

    Offering a solution

Read the following five-paragraph essay that a student wrote about the impact of John Lennon's music. Notice that the first line of each new paragraph is indented. After you have read the entire essay, label the parts on the lines provided.

John Lennon: A Musician for All Time

    Imagine the world without John Lennon; it's almost inconceivable. How can one envision a world without the melodies and lyrics of the man who transformed the way people feel about popular music? John Lennon did not set out to leave an indelible impact on the world. His beginnings were no different from those of thousands of other teenage hopefuls who went from club to club in pursuit of a recording contract. After much hard work, John Lennon and the other members of the Beatles became world famous. But at the pinnacle of his success, Lennon had the courage and vision to move beyond contemporary rock 'n' roll. He broke away from the most popular group of all time and ultimately emerged as his generation's most influential voice. More than any other contemporary artist, Lennon spoke in a universal language that transcended generational lines, combined musical forms, and crossed geographical borders.

Lennon's inspirational music and his persona provided a vehicle for transcending generational divisions that existed while he was alive and still exist today. During the 1960s and 1970s, when Lennon was an active musician, people of all ages admired and responded to his music. So why are so many members of the '90s generation heavily influenced by a '60s musician? Perhaps it is because Lennon speaks to the inner voice in each of us that questions the status quo and strives for a better world. Today, Lennon's music still links his generation to many others.

John Lennon was also a unique artist because of his ability to combine musical forms. Not only did he explore new directions in music, but he embraced them, reinventing himself over and over again, despite offending the millions of fans who mourned the breakup of the Beatles. As he matured as a musician, Lennon incorporated classical music into rock 'n' roll songs. He also added some of the Hindu sound into his compositions. Lennon's music expresses the full range of human emotion, from the introspective mood of "Nowhere Man" to the playful refrain of "Yellow Submarine." Lennon was always surprising his fans with new and creative combinations of musical forms.

John Lennon was tremendously successful in crossing geographical borders through his powerful lyrics, such as those of his song "Imagine." Lennon sang, "I hope that someday you'll join us, and the world will be as one." He suggested that people of all nationalities should join together. He believed in the unification of all people everywhere. As the world becomes a smaller place and geographic borders melt away, the ability to communicate effectively will become vital. Lennon understood this and tried to teach people to get along with one another.

Although John Lennon is no longer with us, his music is still very much a part of people's lives. He was a remarkable individual who spoke in a language that everyone could relate to. During a turbulent time, his optimistic message of peace, love, and happiness emerged. And today, people still refer to the themes of his songs and look to them for answers. Perhaps this is because Lennon was tremendously successful in melting down barriers and borders between people and in finding ways to unify them.

1. The Introduction

Most formal essays begin with an introductory paragraph. In some ways, the introduction is the most important paragraph of your essay. Because it is the first one that will be read, it must capture the attention of the audience and create a desire to read the rest of the essay. It should set the stage for what follows and give the reader an idea of what to expect.

The function of the introduction is
- to **provide background information**,
- to **capture the reader's interest**,
- to **state the thesis.**

While there are no set rules for writing an introduction and you are encouraged to be creative, there are several techniques that have proven successful. Many introductions use one or a combination of the following techniques to provide background information and capture the reader's attention.

A. Move from general to specific

This type of introduction opens with a general statement on the subject that establishes its importance and then leads the reader to the more specific thesis statement.

B. Use an anecdote

Another way to write an introduction is to relate an interesting story that will get the reader interested in the subject. Newspaper and magazine writers frequently use this technique for their articles.

C. Use a quotation

A quotation is an easy way to introduce your topic. You can quote an authority on your subject or use an interesting quotation from an article. You can also be more informal and use a proverb or favorite saying of a friend or relative.

D. Ask a question

Asking one or more questions at the beginning of an essay is a good way to engage the readers in the topic right away. They will want to read on in order to find the answers to the questions.

E. Present facts and statistics

Presenting some interesting facts or statistics on your subject establishes credibility.

ANALYZING INTRODUCTIONS

Reread the introduction for the John Lennon essay on page 40. Notice that the author used several techniques to get the reader interested in the subject. She began with a quote from one of Lennon's most famous songs. She also asked a provocative question to get the reader actively thinking about her topic: *How can one envision a world without the melodies and lyrics of the man who transformed the way people feel about popular music?*

Now read the following sample introductions. Then, in small groups, identify the technique or techniques used in each one. Remember that authors often use a combination of techniques to write an introduction.

1. Karate, which literally means "the art of empty hands," is the most widely practiced of all the martial arts. It is primarily a means of self-defense that uses the body as a weapon for striking, kicking, and blocking. Originating in the ancient Orient, the art of karate is more than 1,000 years old. It developed first as a form of monastic training and later became a method of self-defense. During the seventeenth century, karate became highly developed as an art on the Japanese island of Okinawa. Over the years, this ancient art has gained much popularity, and today karate is practiced throughout the world. More than a method of combat, karate emphasizes self-discipline, positive attitude, and high moral purpose.

Technique(s): _____

_____

2. One student looks at his neighbor's exam paper and quickly copies the answers. Another student finds out the questions on a test before her class takes it and tells her friends. Still another student sneaks a sheet of paper with formulas written on it into the test room. What about you? Would you be tempted to cheat on an exam if you knew you wouldn't get caught? According to a recent national survey, 40 percent of American teenagers would cheat under that condition. What is causing this epidemic of cheating in our schools? Most students cheat on tests because they feel pressure to get into a good college, because they want to avoid the hours of studying they need in order to get high grades, or simply because they are not concerned with honesty.

Technique(s): _____

_____

3. Homicides cause the deaths of more children in Washington, D.C., than any other single type of injury, including car accidents, house fires, or drowning. Unfortunately, this phenomenon is not exclusive to Washington. The overcrowded neighborhoods of many big American cities, such as New York, Detroit, Miami, Chicago, and Los Angeles, are all plagued with senseless violent crime. Types of violent crime range from arson and burglary to assault, rape, and murder. The solution to this growing problem is not to build more and bigger prisons, but rather to examine and deal with the causes: easy access to guns, drug use, and overwhelming poverty.

Technique(s): _____

_____

4. "Misty, a five-month-old German shepherd puppy, goes to the hospital twice a week, but not to see a veterinarian. At this Veteran's Administration Hospital, Misty is helping doctors—not the other way around. In what may seem like a role reversal, animals like Misty are visiting the halls of human illness to relieve a type of pain doctors cannot treat. Their therapy is love, both giving it and helping others return it to them." Pets ranging from dogs to tropical fish are showing up as therapists in hospitals, nursing homes, prisons, and other institutions.
Source: *Cobblestone*, June 1985

Technique(s): _____

_____

5. Experience, not theory, has taught me the truth of the popular saying, "Two heads are better than one." For the past two years, the job of secretary in my office has been shared very successfully by two people. This "job-sharing" arrangement has worked out quite well for all involved. All over the business world, the interest in flexible employment arrangements, like job-sharing, is growing. Employers are beginning to realize that there are many talented people out there who are looking for alternatives to traditional patterns of employment. In a job-sharing arrangement, a full-time job is shared by two people. As an executive in a multinational firm, I feel that job-sharing is one way that organizations can meet the growing diversity of employees' needs. Not only is job-sharing helpful to employees, it also offers several advantages to employers. With two people working together, tasks tend to be completed more quickly, a wider range of skills is brought to the job, and most importantly, production is increased.

Technique(s): _____

_____

Writing Thesis Statements

After you have presented some general background information, you will need to narrow your focus. This is done in a thesis statement, which is often the last sentence of the introduction. A thesis statement is similar to a topic sentence in several ways. Just as a topic sentence controls the information for a paragraph, a thesis statement controls the information for an entire essay.

A good thesis statement

identifies the subject of the essay,

establishes the aspects of the subject that the essay will deal with.

Underline the thesis statement in *John Lennon: A Musician for All Time* on page 40 and answer the following questions:

1. Does the thesis statement identify the subject of the essay?
2. Does it establish the aspects of the subject that the essay develops?

Now look back at the sample introductions on pages 42 and 43 and underline the thesis statement in each one. Write the five thesis statements on the lines below.

1. _____

_____

2. _____

_____

3. _____

_____

4. _____

_____

5. _____

_____

Writing an Introduction

A. Write the introduction for a five-paragraph essay on *the pressures of being a student.* Follow these steps:

1. Spend some time thinking about the angle of the subject that you plan to write about. For example, are you going to discuss the pressures of being a student in a foreign country or in your native country? Are you going to talk about the pressures of a high school student, college student, or graduate student? Other angles you might consider are the pressures of being a student and having a job or being a parent. Are you going to talk about economic, academic, social, or emotional pressures?

2. Decide what technique or techniques you want to use to introduce your subject. Would an anecdote be effective? What about a quote or some facts and statistics?

3. End the introduction with a thesis statement that identifies your subject and establishes the three points you plan to develop in your essay.

_____

_____

_____

_____

_____

_____

_____

_____

_____

_____

4. Read your introduction to the class. Listen to other students' introductions for comparison.

B. Follow the same steps and write introductions for these subjects on a separate piece of paper:

1. Why you chose your major or career
2. The benefits of a large (or small) university

2. The Body

The body of an essay consists of several paragraphs that develop and support the thesis. Each body paragraph develops one point from the thesis statement. These paragraphs all begin with a topic sentence that is supported with specific details, facts, and examples. The body paragraphs of an essay should be arranged in the order that was stated in the thesis statement.

Analyzing Body Paragraphs

Look again at the essay _John Lennon: A Musician for All Time_ on pages 40 and 41. Write the thesis statement here.

_____

_____

_____

What is the topic of the first body paragraph?

_____

_____

Does the topic sentence of that paragraph state its main idea?

_____

(continued on next page)

Does it develop the first point mentioned in the thesis statement?

_____

Is it supported with specific details?

_____

What is the topic of the second body paragraph?

_____

Does the topic sentence of that paragraph state its main idea?

_____

Does it develop the second point mentioned in the thesis statement?

_____

Is it supported with specific details?

_____

What is the topic of the third body paragraph?

_____

Does the topic sentence of that paragraph state its main idea?

_____

Does it develop the third point mentioned in the thesis statement?

_____

Is it supported with specific details?

_____

Writing Body Paragraphs

A. Reread the introduction you wrote on *the pressures of being a student* on page 44. Based on your thesis statement, determine the topic and order of each of the three body paragraphs. Write a topic sentence for each body paragraph on the lines below.

Topic sentence for first body paragraph:

_____

Topic sentence for second body paragraph:

_____

Topic sentence for third body paragraph:

_____

B. On a separate piece of paper, write a first draft of the body paragraphs for the essay on *the pressures of being a student.* Follow the principles you learned in Chapter 2 for writing effective paragraphs. Use the topic sentences you just wrote for each of the three body paragraphs and support them with specific details.

Finding Three Points to Develop Your Subject

It is sometimes difficult to think of three main points for the body paragraphs. However, there are a number of common ways to divide a general subject into three parts. For example, if your general subject is *the effects of computers*, there are several possible ways you could divide it. You might think about *time* and describe the effects of computers in the past, present, and future. Or you might consider *people* and write about the effects on children, adults, and the elderly. Still another way would be to analyze the effects of computers on *society*, economically, educationally, and socially.

The following chart provides additional suggestions for how to divide a broad subject.

Place	People
1. local 2. national 3. international	1. students 2. workers 3. retired people
1. home 2. work 3. school	1. family 2. friends 3. co-workers
1. land 2. sea 3. air	1. children 2. adults 3. the elderly
Time	**Society**
1. past 2. present 3. future	1. economic 2. political 3. social/educational/religious
1. childhood 2. adulthood 3. old age	1. business 2. science 3. the arts

Ready to Write

For each of the following essay topics, think of three main points that you could develop into an essay. You may use ideas from the chart or come up with ideas of your own.

EXAMPLE

Topic: The Effects of Pollution

Main Points: a. _Land_

b. _Water_

c. _Air_

1. Topic: The Benefits of Learning English

Main Points: a. _good job._

b. _make a friend._

c. _learned culture_

2. Topic: The Impact of Natural Disasters

Main Points: a. _____

b. _____

c. _____

3. Topic: The Role of the Media in Our Lives

Main Points: a. _____

b. _____

c. _____

4. Topic: The Changing Role of Women

Main Points: a. _____

b. _____

c. _____

5. Topic: The Causes of Illiteracy

Main Points: a. _____

b. _____

c. _____

Choose one of the five topics above and write a draft of the three body paragraphs on a separate sheet of paper. Exchange papers with a classmate. Read your partner's paragraphs carefully and write an introduction for his or her essay. Return the paper to the original author. Save your paper.

3. The Conclusion

The final paragraph of your essay is the conclusion.

The purpose of this last paragraph is to summarize, without using the same words, the main points you have made in your essay. Your concluding paragraph should also leave your reader agreeing, disagreeing, or at least thinking about your thesis.

Just as there are several ways to write an introduction, there are several common ways to write a conclusion.

A. Summarize your main points

When you use this method of finishing your essay, you simply restate the main points you presented in your essay. Make sure that you do not repeat your words exactly, however. It is essential that you figure out a new way to say them.

B. Ask a question

Writers often want to leave their readers realizing that there is a problem that needs to be solved or an issue that needs to be resolved. A question is a good way of getting your readers' attention and getting them thinking about what can be done.

C. Suggest a solution, offer a recommendation, or make a prediction

Depending on the topic of your essay, the conclusion might be a good place for you to suggest a solution to a problem that you have discussed, or to make a recommendation or a prediction.

Analyzing Conclusions

A. Read the following sample conclusions. In small groups, identify the technique or techniques used in each one.

1. Although John Lennon is no longer with us, his music is still very much a part of people's lives. He was a remarkable individual who spoke in a language that everyone could relate to. During a turbulent time, his optimistic message of peace, love, and happiness emerged. And today, people still refer to the themes of his songs and look to them for answers. Perhaps this is because Lennon was tremendously successful in melting down barriers and borders between people and in finding ways to unify them.

Technique(s): _____

_____

2. In conclusion, although sleep research is a relatively new field, it is a topic arousing considerable interest. A decade ago, only a handful of sleep disorder centers existed; however, today there are more than seventy-five. Consequently, scientists are beginning to unlock the mysteries of what Shakespeare called the "chief nourisher in life's feast." Still, there are numerous chapters to be added to the bedtime story. And then problem sleepers will be able to rest easy.

Source: *Your Health and Fitness*

Technique(s): _____

_____

(continued on next page)

3. During the course of his life, Peter gained a great deal of power and exerted much influence on the course of Russian history. In summary, although he was not always completely successful, he worked very hard to modernize and westernize Russia. Although his actions were not always popular, everything Peter did was in the best interest of his country. By the end of his life, Peter had made significant progress toward achieving his goal of transforming Russia. Therefore, in my opinion, he deserves the name Peter the Great.

Technique(s): _____

_____

4. Technological improvements by aircraft manufacturers are continuing at a healthy pace, and it is no coincidence that the new generation of jets has proved to be the safest planes. With a bit of luck, future airline safety studies will demonstrate what we already know: that flying is the safest way to travel.

Source: *Conde Nast Traveler*

Technique(s): _____

_____

5. Finally, "This wasn't how Diana was meant to be. In the fairy-tale version of royalty, she was meant to produce children—'an heir and a spare,' as they say in Britain—enjoy muddy walks in the country, ride to hounds, be strong and silent, and remain that crucial two steps behind her husband whenever they appeared in public. She wouldn't do it. It's a late-century thing: strong women, with their own agendas, raising uncomfortable questions for old, set-in-their ways institutions. And the British monarchy will never be the same again." Or will it?

Source: *Newsweek*, December 4, 1995

Technique(s): _____

_____

6. As I have shown, low-income senior citizens make up approximately 30 percent of the elderly population. These people are among the most vulnerable members of society because they depend so heavily on government programs for food, shelter, and medical needs. They are the ones who will suffer the most severely if the government cuts back on its social programs.

Technique(s): _____

_____

B. Look through several newspapers and magazines for interesting articles. Cut out three examples each of introductory and concluding paragraphs and bring them to class. In small groups, discuss what makes each paragraph effective or ineffective as an introduction or a conclusion. What techniques did the writers use?

Writing Conclusions

Signals That Introduce a Summary or Conclusion

Note: These signals should be followed by a comma.

therefore	consequently	thus
to summarize	in brief	to conclude
in summary	last of all	finally
in conclusion	in short	

1. Reread the introduction and body paragraphs you wrote on *the pressures of being a student* on pages 44 and 46. Write the conclusion to this essay. Use some of the transition signals from the box.

_____

_____

_____

_____

_____

_____

_____

_____

_____

2. Take out the papers from the exercise you did on page 48. With the same partner, write conclusions for the two essays.

Putting Together the First Draft

On a separate piece of paper, put together the first draft of your entire essay on *the pressures of being a student*. Include the introduction, three supporting paragraphs, and the conclusion. Give your essay a title. Save your paper.

On Your Own

Choose one of the other topics on page 48 and write a five-paragraph essay. Be sure that your essay includes an introduction, a body, and a conclusion.

Chapter Highlights: Crossword Puzzle

ACROSS

2. One way to get your reader's attention is to ask a _____.
4. Paragraphs of an essay that develop and support the thesis
6. A short, interesting, or amusing story about a person or an event
7. To describe something that will happen in the future
8. A paragraph has _____ when all the supporting sentences relate to the topic sentence.
9. States the main idea of the essay and is often the last sentence in the introduction
11. Paragraph of an essay that captures the reader's interest and states the thesis
13. One technique authors use in their conclusion is to make a _____ about the future.
14. To give advice or suggest
17. To restate the main points, using new words
18. Transition words and phrases add _____ to a paragraph and essay.
19. A concluding paragraph often suggests a _____ to a problem.

DOWN

1. The name of an essay is the _____.
2. A _____ is sometimes used at the beginning of an introductory paragraph.
3. A group of sentences about one main topic
4. An introduction gives _____ information to capture the reader's attention.
5. Paragraph of an essay that summarizes the main points
9. Sentence in a paragraph that states the main idea
10. Presenting facts and _____ on a subject helps establish credibility.
12. Another word for *subject* is _____.
15. A set of paragraphs about one subject
16. Your first attempt at writing on a topic

Revising and Editing

It has been said that there is no good writing, only good rewriting. Now that you have practiced the first three steps in the writing process, it is time to turn to the important rewriting steps of revising and editing.

Step Four: Revising

The word *revision* is a combination of the root word *vision* and the prefix *re-*, which means "again." When you revise, you "see again." That is, you look at your writing again to see how you can improve it. What kind of changes should you make as you revise?

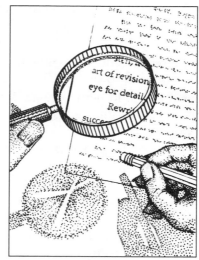

When you revise your writing, you can

- **add new ideas** or more specific support,
- **eliminate irrelevant sentences,**
- **rearrange ideas** to improve the organization.

Practicing Revision

Reread the draft of the essay you wrote on *the pressures of being a student* on page 51. Answer the following questions:

1. What is the subject of your essay?

_____

2. What is the purpose of this essay?

_____

3. Who is your audience?

_____

Revise your essay for support, unity, and coherence by answering each of the following questions.

Revising Checklist

1. Does the introduction create interest in the topic for readers?	___ yes	___ not yet
2. Does the introduction state the main idea of the essay in a clear thesis statement?	___ yes	___ not yet
3. Does the first body paragraph have a topic sentence that states the first main supporting point?	___ yes	___ not yet
4. Does every sentence in that paragraph support the topic sentence?	___ yes	___ not yet
5. Have irrelevant sentences been eliminated?	___ yes	___ not yet
6. Are the sentences arranged in a logical order?	___ yes	___ not yet
7. Are there transitions to guide the reader from one idea to the next?	___ yes	___ not yet
8. Does the second body paragraph have a topic sentence that states the second main supporting point?	___ yes	___ not yet
9. Does every sentence in that paragraph support the topic sentence?	___ yes	___ not yet
10. Have irrelevant sentences been eliminated?	___ yes	___ not yet
11. Are the sentences arranged in a logical order?	___ yes	___ not yet
12. Are there transitions to guide the reader from one idea to the next?	___ yes	___ not yet
13. Does the third body paragraph have a topic sentence that states the third main supporting point?	___ yes	___ not yet
14. Does every sentence in that paragraph support the topic sentence?	___ yes	___ not yet
15. Have irrelevant sentences been eliminated?	___ yes	___ not yet
16. Are the sentences arranged in a logical order?	___ yes	___ not yet
17. Are there transitions to guide the reader from one idea to the next?	___ yes	___ not yet
18. Do the supporting paragraphs provide adequate support and enough specific information to develop and prove the point?	___ yes	___ not yet
19. Does the conclusion summarize the main ideas of the essay?	___ yes	___ not yet
20. Does the title of the essay give readers a good idea of what it will be about?	___ yes	___ not yet

If the answer to any of the questions is "not yet," go back and try to improve your essay.

Pair Work

Sometimes it is helpful to have someone else read your paper and offer suggestions on ways to improve it. Exchange papers with a classmate and read each other's essay. Use the following questions as a guide for suggesting improvements in your partner's essay:

1. What are the strengths of this essay? What did you like best about it?
2. What weaknesses did you notice? What suggestions can you offer to improve them?

Read your partner's suggestions. Decide which suggestions you agree with. Write a revised draft of your essay.

Step Five: Editing

The final step of the writing process is editing. When you edit a paragraph or essay, you check to make sure that the grammar, spelling, capitalization, and punctuation are correct.

Here is a review of some things to check when you edit your writing.

Punctuation

Punctuation marks, such as commas, periods, and quotation marks, help readers interpret sentences. They determine how a sentence should be read and understood. Like most languages, English has certain rules of punctuation. The guidelines below will help you master some of the most important ones.

PERIOD

- Use a period at the end of a statement:

    Argentina's economy is a mix of agriculture and industry.

- Use a period with most abbreviations:

Mr.	A.M.
Mrs.	P.M.
apt.	assoc.
M.A.	

QUESTION MARK

- Use a question mark at the end of a direct question:

    Who is going to drive me to the airport?

COMMA

- Use a comma to separate words or phrases in a series:

    The sea around Antarctica is home to dolphins, porpoises, whales, seals, and other sea creatures.

- Use a comma to separate independent clauses joined by a coordinating conjunction:

    We left in plenty of time, but we still missed the bus.
    I worked hard all day, so I went to bed early.

- Use a comma after many introductory phrases or clauses:

    Working late into the night, I drank several cups of strong coffee.

- Use a comma before a direct quote:

    Christina said, "The train leaves in half an hour."

- Use a comma between the day of the month and the year:

    August 15, 1983

- Use a comma to separate cities from states:

    Billings, Montana
    Tallahassee, Florida

COLON

- Use a colon to introduce a series:

    Consumer products can be classified into three categories: convenience products, shopping products, and specialty products.

- Use a colon to introduce a long or formal quotation:

    Writing about his life, British philosopher Bertrand Russell said: "Three passions, simple but overwhelmingly strong, have governed my life: the longing for love, the search for knowledge, and the unbearable pity for the suffering of mankind."

Note: The first colon is used to introduce the quotation; the second one introduces a series.

- Use a colon to separate hours from minutes:

    3:15
    6:45

- Use a colon after the salutation in a formal letter:

    Dear Dr. Brody:
    Dear Ms. Rosen:

QUOTATION MARKS

- Use quotation marks to enclose a direct quote:

    Jorge said, "I have already finished my homework."

- Use quotation marks to identify titles of songs, short stories, poems, articles, essays, and chapters from a book. (Underline the titles of longer works such as books and newspapers. If you are using a computer, the titles of longer works should be in italic type.)

    My favorite song is "Imagine" by John Lennon.

Practicing Punctuation

Punctuate the following sentences:

1. He was born on April 22 1981 in Portland Oregon
2. How many books have you read lately
3. We will have to leave by 530 PM
4. Dr Anderson has a very full schedule today

5. I just finished reading Hemingway's novel The Old Man and the Sea
6. Most people like chocolate but Jane is allergic to it
7. The restaurant has three specialties grilled steak marinated chicken and fried shrimp
8. In conclusion Mario Vargas Llosa is one of the greatest writers of the twentieth century
9. Marion said I can't go with you because I have too much homework
10. I think that Pablo Neruda's poem If You Forget Me is the most beautiful poem I've ever read

Capitalization

The following rules summarize the main uses of capitalization in English. If you are not sure when to capitalize a word, you should use your dictionary as a reference.

- Capitalize the first word of a sentence:

    Fishing is an important industry in Peru.

- Capitalize all proper nouns and names. Capitalize a title that precedes a name:

    Dr. Lourie
    Professor Cantor

- Capitalize the names of racial and ethnic groups:

    African-American
    Asian
    Caucasian

(Exception: Do not capitalize the words *black* or *white* when referring to racial groups.)

- Capitalize the names of specific geographical locations including countries, cities, towns, rivers, streets, and mountains:

    Paris
    Juniper Avenue
    Mount Rushmore

- Capitalize the days of the week, months, and holidays:

    Tuesday
    September
    Christmas

- Capitalize the names of religions:

    Buddhism
    Christianity

- Capitalize nationalities and languages:

    Japanese
    Arabic

- Capitalize all words in a title except articles, prepositions, and conjunctions, unless they are the first or the last word in the title:

    Gone with the Wind
    For Whom the Bell Tolls
    The Sun Also Rises

Practicing Capitalization

Capitalize each of the following sentences correctly:

1. my russian history teacher is very handsome.
2. have you read <u>romeo and juliet</u> in your english literature class yet?
3. i meet with my advisor every tuesday and thursday morning.
4. my sister, ruth, has just returned from a trip to cairo and tel aviv.
5. ninety-eight percent of all turks are moslem.

Punctuation and Capitalization Review

Add the correct capitalization and punctuation to the sentences that follow:

1. traffic is causing serious pollution in some cities such as athens mexico city and los angeles
2. when will professor klein be in his office
3. my favorite poem is fire and ice by robert frost
4. i'll meet you on tuesday afternoon at 430 in front of the library on liberty street
5. mrs baker is one of the most inspiring speakers i've ever heard
6. the earliest maps anyone knows of were made by babylonians and egyptians over 4,000 years ago
7. the himalayas are the world's highest mountains
8. maria asked what time does the movie casablanca start
9. in 1980 george shaller a world-famous wildlife biologist began researching the panda in its natural habitat
10. professor dickens is sick so his tuesday night class will be canceled

Sentence Fragments

Every English sentence must have a subject and a verb. It must also express a complete thought. A complete sentence can stand alone. That is, it makes sense by itself. If a sentence lacks either a subject or a verb or is not a complete thought, it is called a ***sentence fragment.***

EXAMPLES:

1. Lack-of-Subject Fragment

   Fragment: Did very well on her math exam.

   Complete Sentence: Georgette did very well on her math exam.

2. Lack-of-Verb Fragment

   Fragment: Both Alexander and his younger sister Lisa.

   Complete Sentence: Both Alexander and his younger sister Lisa enjoy tennis.

3. Dependent Clause Fragment

   Fragment: Before I went to college.

   Complete Sentence: Before I went to college, I worked part-time at a bank.

A dependent clause is often confused with a complete sentence because it contains a subject and a verb. However, it is not a complete thought. A dependent clause must be attached to an independent clause to form a complete sentence with a complete thought. Following is a list of the common words that are used to begin dependent clauses:

when	while	since
before	after	as
because	if	unless
until	although	though
even though	even if	despite
in spite of	whereas	so that
who	whom	whose
whatever	whenever	wherever
where		

Read the following example:

> Because the meteorologist predicted rain.

Although this clause has a subject and verb, it is not a complete sentence. It does not make sense by itself.

There are two possible ways to correct this mistake:

1. Make the dependent clause a complete sentence by removing the word *Because.*

   Sentence fragment: Because the meteorologist predicted rain.

   Complete sentence: The meteorologist predicted rain.

2. Attach the dependent clause to an independent clause.

   Sentence fragment: Because the meteorologist predicted rain.

   Complete sentence: Because the meteorologist predicted rain, I took my umbrella

   with me.

Correcting Sentence Fragments

Write *C* in front of each *complete sentence*. Write *F* in front of each *sentence fragment*. Then rewrite the fragments so that they are complete sentences.

_____ 1. Works out in the gym every day.

_____

_____ 2. I love Monet's gardens in Giverny because gardening is my hobby.

_____

_____ 3. Hockey a very dangerous sport if you don't have the right equipment.

_____

_____ 4. Because I couldn't understand the homework.

_____

(continued on next page)

_____ 5. And ran out of gas on the way to work.

_____ 6. Whenever my next-door neighbor has time.

_____ 7. Although she had a bad cold and hadn't slept well for days.

_____ 8. That my friend told me was the best movie he had ever seen.

Write a sentence using each of the following words.

1. after

2. although

3. because

4. before

5. if

6. since

7. unless

8. when

9. until

10. despite

Exchange sentences with a classmate. Check your partner's sentences. Are they all complete sentences?

Run-on Sentences

A run-on sentence occurs when two complete sentences are written as one sentence.

EXAMPLE:

> Sue loves to cook she is always in the kitchen.

There are three ways to correct this problem:

1. Use punctuation, usually a period, to separate the two sentences.

    Run-on sentence: Sue loves to cook she is always in the kitchen.

    Correct sentences: Sue loves to cook. She is always in the kitchen.

2. Use a coordinating conjunction *(and, but, for, so, or, nor, yet)* to connect the two clauses.

    Run-on sentence: The movie was boring we watched it anyway.

    Correct sentence: The movie was boring, but we watched it anyway.

3. Use a subordinating conjunction to connect the two clauses.

    Run-on sentence: I am very hungry I didn't eat breakfast.

    Correct sentence: I am very hungry because I didn't eat breakfast.

Correcting Run-on Sentences

Write *C* in front of each *complete sentence*. Write *R* in front of each *run-on sentence*. Then correct the run-on sentences.

_____ 1. I like my dentist he is very gentle.

_____

_____ 2. My son bought two T-shirts he thought they were so cool.

_____

_____ 3. It was too cold yesterday to ski we stayed in the lodge all day.

_____

_____ 4. When Jerry finishes work, he'll join us at the party.

_____

_____ 5. The Pilgrims first came to Plymouth, Massachusetts, in 1620 they were seeking religious freedom.

_____

_____ 6. If all twenty-five of us agree, it will be a miracle.

_____

_____ 7. Dennis called to say that his computer is making strange noises he thinks it is broken.

_____

(continued on next page)

_____ 8. They wanted to play golf but we thought it was too hot we all went swimming instead.

_____

_____ 9. There are several ways to get from New York to Philadelphia the most convenient is by train.

_____

_____ 10. I have a very good memory my husband, on the other hand, does not.

_____

Agreement of Subjects and Verbs

You already know that every English sentence must have a subject and a verb. In order for a sentence to be grammatically correct, the subject and verb must agree with each other. This means that if the subject is singular, the verb must be singular. If the subject is plural, the verb must be plural.

EXAMPLE:

> My friend was late for class.
> My friends were late for class.

KEEP THE FOLLOWING RULES IN MIND:

- Subjects that are joined by *and* usually take a plural verb:

  My friend and I **were** late for class.

- Subjects that are joined by *or* and *nor* take a verb that agrees with the subject that is closer to the verb:

  Either Jason or Pat **drives** me to school.
  Either Jason or his parents **drive** me to school.

In the first sentence, *Pat* is closer to the verb. Because *Pat* is singular, the verb must be singular. In the second sentence, *his parents* is closer to the verb, so the verb must be plural:

  Neither Ann nor Emily **plans** to join the tennis club.
  Neither Ann nor her sisters **plan** to join the tennis club.

In the first sentence, *Ann* is closer to the verb. Because *Ann* is singular, the verb must be singular. In the second sentence, *her sisters* is closer to the verb, so the verb must be plural.

- A subject must agree with the verb even when other words come between them:

> This new book of poems **is** by Daniel Lewis.
> The poems in this book **are** by Daniel Lewis.

The subject of the first sentence is *book,* which is singular. The subject of the second sentence is *poems,* which is plural.

- The following words are singular and take singular verbs:

one	nobody	nothing	each
anyone	anybody	anything	either
someone	somebody	something	neither
everyone	everybody	everything	

> Each of the students **is** required to write a five-paragraph essay. (*Each* is the subject)

> Everybody **wants** to start the movie now.

- The following words are plural and take plural verbs:

both	others
few	several
many	

> Several of the students **are** required to write five-paragraph essays. (*Several* is the subject)

> Others **want** to start the movie later.

- Expressions of time, money, measurement, weight, and fractions are singular and take singular verbs:

> Twenty-five dollars **seems** like a reasonable price for this sweater.
> Twelve inches **equals** one foot.
> **Three-fourths** is more than one-half.

Circle the correct verb for each of the following sentences:

1. One of my friends (has/have) a new car.
2. Everyone who works hard in this class (do/does) well.
3. Many of my friends (like/likes) the professor.
4. The instructor (don't/doesn't) give a lot of homework.
5. One of the reasons that I chose to go into medicine (is/are) that I like to work with people.
6. Fifty dollars (is/are) too much to spend on dinner at this restaurant.
7. Both Jane and her cousins (go/goes) to the University of Michigan.
8. The book and the movie (has/have) the same ending.

Agreement of Possessive Pronouns

Just as a subject and verb must agree, a possessive pronoun must also agree with the word it refers to. If the word referred to is singular, the possessive pronoun must be singular. If the word is plural, the possessive pronoun must be plural.

> The little **boy** is holding **his** mother's hand.
> The **children** are holding **their** mother's hands.
> **Each** of the girls had **her** own bedroom in the apartment.
> **Both** of our daughters have **their** own cars.

Circle the correct possessive pronoun for each of the following sentences:

1. Both of the students forgot (his/their) notebooks.
2. Neither of my sisters owns (her/their) own house.
3. Matthew likes (his/their) meat cooked well-done.
4. The Wexlers send (his/their) children to private school.
5. None of the women has retired from (her/their) job.

You Be the Editor

Read the following passage. Then figure out how and where to divide it into several correct sentences. You will need to make some word changes, add punctuation, and correct capitalization. Write the corrected paragraph below.

how could I have been so stupid as to let my car run out of gas on the interstate when I was in a hurry to get to work on time and there was no gas station in sight and no hope unless I got lucky and a kind person with a car phone came along and saw me sitting there and called for help but guess what that's what happened so I was only twenty minutes late for work but it would have been more if that nice man hadn't come along.

_____

_____

_____

_____

_____

_____

_____

_____

_____

_____

_____

_____

Pair Work

Exchange papers with a classmate. Compare your corrected version with your partner's. Notice that the passage can be corrected in more than one way.

Practicing Editing

Look over the revised draft of your essay on *the pressures of being a student* (see page 54) and answer the following questions:

Editing Checklist		
1. Is the first sentence of each new paragraph indented?	___ yes	___ not yet
2. Does the first word of each sentence begin with a capital letter?	___ yes	___ not yet
3. Is the punctuation correct in all the sentences?	___ yes	___ not yet
4. Are all the sentences complete sentences? That is, does each have a subject and a verb and express a complete thought?	___ yes	___ not yet
5. Have you eliminated run-on sentences?	___ yes	___ not yet
6. Have you used the correct verb tense throughout your draft?	___ yes	___ not yet
7. Do you have agreement of subjects and verbs?	___ yes	___ not yet
8. Do you have agreement of nouns and possessive pronouns?	___ yes	___ not yet
9. Have you used correct word order in all your sentences?	___ yes	___ not yet
10. Are all your words spelled correctly?	___ yes	___ not yet

If the answer to any of the questions is "not yet," go back and try to improve your essay. Write the edited draft of your essay on a separate piece of paper.

Writing and Revising an Article

You are going to write an article for the travel section of a newspaper. The focus of your article will be how to plan a trip that will be economical, educational, and fun.

GROUP WORK

It is often easier to write after you have talked about the subject with some other people. In small groups, discuss ways to make travel economical, educational, and fun. Write the ideas that your group discusses in the chart below:

Economical	Educational	Fun

Now complete the following steps as you draft your article:

a. Prewriting

1. Individually or with your classmates, brainstorm a list of ideas for your article.

2. Group the items on the list that go together.

3. Cross out items that do not belong.

b. Planning
On a separate piece of paper, make an informal outline of your essay.

c. Drafting
On a separate piece of paper, write the first draft of your article.

d. Revising
Let a classmate read the first draft of your article to make suggestions about how to revise it. He/She should use the revising checklist on page 54 as a guide.

e. Editing
Make the final corrections on your article, using the editing checklist on page 65 as a guide. Pay attention to the final appearance of the article. Make sure that your handwriting is legible or that your typing is neat and error-free. Give a clean copy of your article to a friend or classmate to read before you hand it in to your teacher.

You Be the Editor

The following paragraph contains nine mistakes. Find the mistakes and correct them. Then copy the corrected paragraph onto a separate sheet of paper.

Wall Street is a narrow, winding street that is less than one Mile long. Despite the fact that is a tiny street, Wall Street is one of the most influential and best-known streets in the world. To most people, Wall Street is synonymous with the New York Stock Exchange and the world of stocks bonds and securities. Because of its location on a thriving and busy harbor at the southern tip of manhattan island. The Wall Street area has historically been an important area for business and trade. It's convenient location made its growth as a center of finance natural. Over the years, Wall Street has become an international symbol of power and high finance. Its name brings to mind power and the excitement of the stock market and its economic, political, and personal impact is felt daily by millions of people all over the world.

Process

Both paragraphs and essays can be organized according to several different patterns. As a writer, it is important for you to select a pattern of organization that fits your purpose. The following summarizes some of the basic patterns of organization and their purposes:

Pattern of Organization	Purpose
Process	to describe the sequence of steps in a procedure
Classification	to describe the logical divisions of a topic or the parts of an object
Cause/Effect	to analyze the causes or effects of a situation
Comparison/Contrast	to show the qualities that are similar or different between two things
Problem/Solution	to describe a problem and evaluate possible solutions

Pair Work

With a classmate, discuss which pattern of organization you would use to write an essay for each of the following purposes:

1. To analyze why a recent presidential campaign was unsuccessful

   _____

2. To discuss the reasons you decided to major in business

   _____

3. To suggest ways to solve the problem of high unemployment in your country

   _____

4. To explain how to install a program in your computer

   _____

5. To describe the types of friends you have

   _____

6. To evaluate the differences between two treatments for back pain

_____

7. To teach your co-workers how to use a new copy machine

_____

8. To describe the categories of movie ratings

_____

Process

When your purpose in writing is to inform your readers about how to do something or to describe the order of steps in a procedure, you will use a **process pattern of organization.** For instance, when you explain procedures such as how to train a dog to do tricks, how to give a good haircut, or how to study for a math test, you are describing steps in a process. You should organize these steps according to time order.

In academic writing, the process pattern of organization is especially important in scientific and technical fields. For example, it is used to describe biological processes such as cell division, chemical processes such as photosynthesis, and technical processes such as how a diesel engine works.

The Language of Process: Useful Phrases and Sentence Patterns

The following transition words indicate the order of steps in a process:

first	the third step	as	soon afterward
the first step	after that	while	from then on
then	before	when	the last step
next	after	meanwhile	finally
the next step			

The following sentence patterns are useful in writing topic sentences and thesis statements for process paragraphs and essays:

1. **It is** | easy / simple / not difficult | **to** _____ **if you have the right** | tools. / equipment. / materials. / ingredients.

   It is easy to change a flat tire if you have the right equipment.

2. _____ **is easy when you follow** | these steps. / these directions. / these instructions. / this procedure.

   Making a delicious omelet is easy when you follow these steps.

3. **There are** $\left|\begin{array}{l}\text{three}\\\text{four}\\\text{several}\end{array}\right|$ **major steps involved in** _____ .

There are three *major steps involved in* studying for an exam.

Write a thesis statement for a process essay on each of the following essay topics. Use a variety of sentence patterns.

1. Topic: How to impress your teacher or boss

   Thesis statement: _____

   _____

2. Topic: How to build a tree house

   Thesis statement: _____

   _____

3. Topic: How to make a pizza

   Thesis statement: _____

   _____

4. Topic: The best way to lose weight

   Thesis statement: _____

   _____

5. Topic: How to make a beautiful flower arrangement

   Thesis statement: _____

   _____

Describing the Steps in a Process

You have just made a bookcase in a woodworking class. Now you need to write a one-paragraph description of the process for your teacher. Look at the step-by-step drawings below.

1) Assemble: wood, nails, glue, a hammer, a saw, sandpaper, and paint.

2) Cut: 2 side pieces 11⁵⁄₈" by 28"
3 pieces for top, bottom, and shelf, 11⁵⁄₈" by 13½"
1 back piece 15" by 28"
two 10" molding strips

3) Sand each piece of wood.

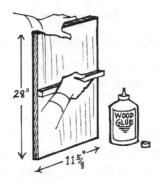

4) Glue one molding strip to each side piece, 14" down from top.

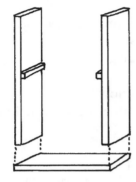

5) Nail side pieces to bottom.

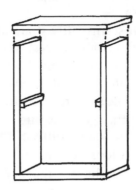

6) Nail the top in place.

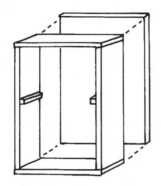

7) Nail the back piece in place.

8) Paint the bookcase and shelf.

9) Let dry 2 hours.

10) Slide the shelf into place.

On a separate piece of paper, write a one-paragraph description of the process. Use the drawings as a guide. Be sure to include a topic sentence that states your purpose and include transition signals to indicate the order of the steps.

Writing a Process Paragraph

Read the following conversation between a student and a librarian.

STUDENT: Excuse me. I'm doing research for a paper I'm writing on the effects of global warming. Can you tell me how to find some current articles on this subject?

LIBRARIAN: Certainly. The best place to begin is over here in the reference section. Are you familiar with how to use the computerized card catalog?

STUDENT: Not really. I've only used it once and I think I've forgotten how it works.

LIBRARIAN: It's really quite easy. All you need to do is type in your topic here and press the return key. The computer will search its database of magazines and journals and give you a list of all the articles related to your topic. You can choose which ones you want to look up, and you can print out the list of citations.

STUDENT: OK. That seems fairly straightforward. But my professor said we could only use articles from the past three years.

LIBRARIAN: That's no problem. The dates of the articles are given right here, so you can just look up the most recent ones.

STUDENT: That's great. Is there anything else I need to know?

LIBRARIAN: Well, another good feature of this program is that it gives you a brief summary of the main points of the article.

STUDENT: How can I look at that?

LIBRARIAN: Just click on the box that says *abstract*. Here, I'll show you.

STUDENT: This sure beats looking through piles of magazines for the right information. Thank you so much for helping me.

LIBRARIAN: You're welcome. If you have any more questions, I'll be at the reference desk.

STUDENT: Oh, one more thing before you go. Where are the magazines and journals?

LIBRARIAN: They are in the periodical section on the second floor. You can't take them out, but there are several copy machines in that area if you need to make a copy of any of the articles.

STUDENT: Thanks again.

Using information from the conversation, write a paragraph about how to use a computerized index to do research. Write your paragraph on a separate piece of paper.

Analyzing a Process Essay

"Wow! How long did it take you to train him to do that?"

Read the essay "How to Train Your Pet," and answer the questions that follow.

How to Train Your Pet

Have you ever wondered how the animals you see on TV and in movies are trained to perform such amazing tricks? Many of their trainers use a technique based on the teaching methods developed by behavioral psychologists such as B. F. Skinner. Skinner studied techniques for reinforcing desired behaviors in animals. Animals can be taught many sophisticated tricks using Skinner's techniques. If you want to teach your pet to do a trick, you must understand the technique psychologists call "shaping." Shaping means reinforcing, or strengthening, behaviors that you want to encourage. Here is how you can use his techniques to train your pet to do tricks.

The first thing you must do is choose your subject. You can pick any household pet, such as a cat, hamster, parrot, or dog. For example, suppose you want to teach your dog to do a trick. Next, choose a reward. Food is usually the easiest reward to use. Keep in mind that in order for food to be an effective reward, your dog has to be hungry. Don't try to teach him a new trick right after he has eaten a big meal. Also, a reward is most effective when it is given at the same time that the dog performs the desired trick. Since you will not always be able to give the dog food as quickly as you would like to, you will need to develop a "conditioned reinforcer." You can do this by connecting the food with something else, such as ringing a bell. In this case, the sound the bell makes is the conditioned reinforcer.

You are now ready to begin conditioning the dog to respond to the bell. Get out about 40 small dog biscuits. Toss a few of them to your dog, one at a time, at a rate of about one or two biscuits a minute. As soon as the dog begins eating the biscuits, ring the bell and then throw him another biscuit. Wait about 30 seconds and then repeat the steps. When you ring the bell, do not make any other sound or movement. Give the biscuit only when the dog is standing in the place where he gets his food. When your dog reaches the point where he goes to the food place whenever you ring the bell, you are ready to begin teaching him the trick.

At this point, you need to choose the trick you want to teach. An easy trick is teaching your dog to roll over. Shape the dog's behavior by reinforcing anything that resembles the behavior you are trying to teach. Begin by reinforcing any attempt to lie down. Then reinforce any movement of his body when he is lying down. Every time you reinforce any of his behaviors that resembles rolling over, immediately give him a biscuit and ring the bell. In this way, he will begin to associate the sound of the bell with the trick. Continue reinforcing closer approximations of rolling over with the biscuits and the bell. During the teaching session, do not touch the dog, talk to him, or in any way distract him. A normal dog, according to Skinner, will learn the trick within five minutes.

As you can see, it is really not very difficult to train your pet to do a trick. It is only a matter of a little time and some effort. Once you have established a conditioned reinforcer, you can easily teach your dog a new trick by shaping his behavior. Remember, though, that if you want to teach your dog another trick, you must eliminate the first behavior by no longer reinforcing it. Eventually, he will stop rolling over and will be ready to learn something new.

Pair Work

Answer the following questions with a classmate:

1. What technique does the author use to introduce the topic?
2. What process is the author describing?
3. How does the author organize the information?
4. Make a list of the steps in the process.

_____

_____

_____

_____

_____

5. What transition words did the author use to achieve coherence? Underline them in the essay.
6. What audience do you think the author had in mind when he wrote this essay?

Essay Plan: Process

The guidelines below will help you remember what you need to do in each part of a process essay.

Introduction

1. State what the process is and why it is important.
2. Define the process.
3. State the purpose for explaining the process.
4. List any equipment, ingredients, or supplies needed to perform the process.

Supporting Paragraphs

1. Describe the steps in the process, using time order.
2. If there are a lot of steps, group them into several main categories.

Conclusion

1. Review why the process is important.
2. Summarize the main steps in the process.

Writing a Process Essay

In this activity, you will practice writing an essay that describes the steps in a process. Follow these steps:

a. Prewriting
Choose one of the following topics and make a list of the steps in the process in the space on the next page.

1. How to get a date with someone who doesn't like you
2. How to study for an exam
3. How to break up with your boyfriend or girlfriend

4. How to drive your teacher crazy
5. How to get fired from your job
6. Your own topic

b. Planning

Organize your list according to time order in the space below. On a separate piece of paper, prepare an informal outline of your essay.

c. Drafting

On a separate piece of paper, write the first draft of your essay. Refer to the essay plan on page 74 to help you draft your essay. Be sure to provide some background information about the process in the introduction and include a clear thesis statement of purpose. Describe the steps in the supporting paragraphs and organize them according to time order. End with a conclusion that summarizes the steps and restates the purpose.

d. Personal Revising

Put your essay away for at least one day. Then use the checklist on page 54 to revise the first draft. Be sure that all your paragraphs are unified and coherent. Also, check to make sure you have adequately described each step in the process. Write or type a revised version of your essay.

e. Peer Revising

Exchange your draft with a classmate. Use the following guide to help improve your partner's essay:

1. What are the strengths of the essay?
2. Did the introduction identify the process and state why it is important?
3. What weaknesses, if any, did you notice in the organization?
4. What suggestions can you offer to improve the organization?
5. Did the author include enough transitions to guide you from one step to the next?
6. Was each step in the process adequately explained?
7. Did the author include an effective conclusion? If not, how can it be improved?

Incorporate any suggestions your partner has made that you agree with.

(continued on next page)

f. Editing

Use the checklist on page 65 to edit your essay. Correct all the grammar, punctuation, capitalization, and spelling errors before you copy it over or type it.

(You) Be the Editor

The following recipe is an example of a process paragraph. The content of the recipe is correct, but there are seven editorial mistakes. Find the mistakes and correct them. Then copy the corrected paragraph on a separate piece of paper.

Recipe

If you like to eat or bake delicious cookies, you will love this recipe. Soften 1/2 pound of butter and mix it together with 2 cups off sugar. Stir in 3 beaten egg and 9 tablespoons of lemon juice. Then add 4 cups of flour 1 teaspoon of baking powder and 2-1/2 teaspoons of nutmeg. As soon as the mixture is thoroughly combined, form the dough into a large ball and refrigerator it for at least 1 hour. When you are ready to bake the cookies, divide the ball of dough in half. Roll the dough out so that is 1/8 inch thick. It will be easier if you use a rolling pin. Cut the cookies into shapes, using the open end of a glass or cookie cutters if you have them. Put the cookies on greased cookie sheets and bake them at 375 degrees for 6 minutes. To make them sweeter and more festive, frost them with colored frosting. With this recipe, the hardest part is trying not to eat to many!

On Your Own

Choose one of the following topics and write a process essay. Make sure that your introduction states the process and your purpose for explaining it. Remember to organize the steps of the process according to time order.

1. How to get an extension on an assignment for school
2. How to apply to a university in your country or the United States
3. How to make up after an argument

Classification

If your purpose in writing is to describe the logical divisions of a topic, you will use a **classification pattern of organization.** When you classify, you group similar items into categories. For example, you could classify news articles into three categories: local, national, and international. Kinds of burns could be classified as first degree, second degree, and third degree. You could classify energy into three types: nuclear, hydraulic, and solar.

Classification is one of the most common patterns of organization in academic writing. In a business class, you might be asked to classify and discuss the various types of insurance policies. In a political science class, you might need to describe the three branches of the U. S. government. In a chemistry class, you might have to categorize all the types of chemical reactions.

There is often more than one way to divide something into several categories. For example, you might classify clothing into three groups: formal clothes, semiformal clothes, and casual clothes. Or you might classify clothing into two groups: indoor wear and outdoor wear. Transportation could also be divided several ways:

a. local, national, international
b. private, public
c. land, air, sea

The way you choose to divide your topic depends on your purpose.

The important thing to remember when you classify is that the categories must be mutually exclusive. In other words, the categories cannot overlap. For example, you could not classify clothing into formal clothes, casual clothes, and summer clothes because the categories overlap. Some summer clothes are formal and others are casual.

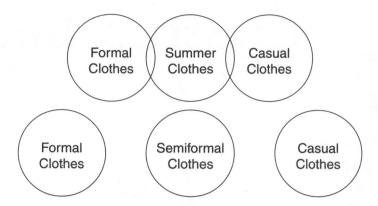

In our original classification of formal clothes, semiformal clothes, and casual clothes, the three categories are mutually exclusive.

The Language of Classification: Useful Sentence Patterns

The following sentence patterns are useful in writing topic sentences and thesis statements for classification paragraphs and essays:

1. **There are** | three | kinds | **of** _____.
            two | types
            four | classes
            several

There are *three kinds* ***of*** *energy: nuclear, hydraulic, and solar.*

2. **We can** | divide | _____ | **into three** | parts:
           classify | | | groups: _____.
           group | | | types:
           categorize | | | kinds:

We can *divide the students in my class* ***into three*** *groups: Asian, European, and South American.*

3. _____ **can be** | divided | **into** | three parts:
                 classified | | two groups: _____.
                 grouped | | three types:
                 categorized | | kinds:
                 | | categories:

News articles ***can be*** *divided* ***into*** *three categories: local, national, and international.*

Practicing Classification

How many ways can you think of to divide the students in your school? Make a list. Identify your method of classification and the groups you can divide students into.

EXAMPLE:

Method of classification: <u>level of proficiency in English</u> _____

       Groups: a. <u>beginning</u> _____

                 b. <u>intermediate</u> _____

                 c. <u>advanced</u> _____

a. Method of classification: _____

    Groups: _____

    _____

    _____

b. Method of classification: _____

    Groups: _____

    _____

    _____

c. Method of classification: _____

    Groups: _____

    _____

    _____

d. Method of classification: _____

    Groups: _____

    _____

    _____

1. Based on your list, write sentences of classification, using a variety of sentence patterns. Refer to the sentence patterns on page 78.

EXAMPLE:

The students in my school can be divided into three levels according to their proficiency in English: beginning, intermediate, and advanced.

a. _____

    _____

b. _____

    _____

c. _____

    _____

d. _____

    _____

2. For each of the following topics, write a sentence of classification. Use a variety of sentence patterns.

EXAMPLE:

Topic: Restaurants in my city

Sentence of classification: *The restaurants in my city can be divided into three groups: fast-food restaurants, family-style restaurants, and gourmet restaurants.*

a. Topic: Courses I have taken

Sentence of classification: _____

_____

b. Topic: Successful people

Sentence of classification: _____

_____

c. Topic: Friends I have had

Sentence of classification: _____

_____

d. Topic: Automobile drivers

Sentence of classification: _____

_____

e. Topic: Television shows

Sentence of classification: _____

_____

Writing a Classification Paragraph

Choose one of the topics from the preceding activity and write a paragraph. Follow these steps:

A. On a separate piece of paper, make an informal outline of your ideas. Include examples of each category in your classification.

B. Write a draft of your paragraph.

C. Revise and edit your draft.

D. Write or type the final copy of your paragraph.

Analyzing a Classification Essay

Read the essay below and answer the questions that follow.

The Marketing Mix

The goal of marketing is to create a product which satisfies the needs of the consumers. Marketers deal with many variables as they work to meet this goal. These variables are called the "marketing mix." All of the variables of the marketing mix can be classified into four basic groups: product, place, promotion, and price. These groups are also known as the "four Ps."

The first "P", product, is concerned with developing a product that will meet the needs of the consumer. This group of variables includes decisions about the product's design, brand name, and packaging. The product does not have to be a physical commodity such as a book or a television. The product can be a service, such as doing someone's laundry or cleaning their house. Whether the product is a physical commodity or a service, it must satisfy the needs of the consumer or else no one will want to buy it.

The second "P", place, is concerned with getting the product to a place where the consumer can easily purchase it. A product is of little use if it is sold at a place where the consumer cannot get to it easily. A product reaches customers through a channel of distribution. This is the system of people and firms that take part in the process of getting the goods and services from the producer to the consumers. The product often goes through several middlemen on its journey from the producer to the consumer. If the product is a physical commodity, then decisions about transportation and storage must be considered.

The third "P", promotion, involves telling consumers why they should buy a certain product. Promotion can be done by personal selling or mass selling. Personal selling takes place when sellers communicate directly to consumers, either in person or over the phone. Mass selling involves the seller's communicating with a large number of consumers at the same time. Television commercials are a major example of mass selling. Another form of promotion is sales promotion. Sales promotion stimulates the interest of consumers with coupons, free samples, contests, and catalogs.

The final "P" is price. Decisions about price involve the seller's trying to figure out the price at which the most consumers will buy a particular product. Sellers must consider the cost of producing the product, the cost of distributing the product, and the cost of promoting the product when they set its price.

The "four Ps" are all connected to each other. They are also each equally important in determining the marketing mix. The products which are the most successful are those which best address the needs of the consumer through some combination of the marketing mix: product, place, promotion, and price.

Pair Work

Answer the following questions with a partner:

1. What is the thesis statement of the essay?
2. What are the four main groups of the marketing mix?
3. What examples does the author use to describe each category?
4. What transitions did the author use to achieve coherence? Underline them in the essay.

The guidelines below will help you remember what you need to do in each part of a classification essay.

Introduction

1. Provide background information about the topic to be classified.
2. Describe how you are going to divide the topic into groups.
3. Give the number of groups and a name for each one.
4. Explain the purpose for the classification.

Supporting Paragraphs

1. Identify and describe one category in each supporting paragraph.
2. Explain the common characteristics of the members of each category.
3. Give examples of items in each category.

Conclusion

1. Restate the method of classification.
2. Summarize the categories.

Completing a Classification Essay

You are a meteorologist. You have been asked to write an article describing the three main categories of clouds for your city's science museum. Here is the introductory paragraph that you have written for the article:

> The scientific study of clouds began in 1803 when Luke Howard, a British pharmacist and amateur meteorologist, introduced the first system for classifying clouds. Although many other procedures for cloud classification have been devised over the years, Howard's system is so simple and effective that it is still in use today. It is based on the shape, distribution, and altitude of clouds. He identified ten different categories, but they are all variations of three basic cloud forms. Howard used their Latin names to identify them: *cirrus* (meaning "curl"), *stratus* ("spreading out in layers or sheets"), and *cumulus* ("a pile or heap").

Now you need to write the three supporting paragraphs. Here is the information you will use as the basis for these three paragraphs. There is a lot of information, so you will have to decide which items you want to include.

Cirrus

Stratus

Cumulus

Cirrus Clouds

– found about 5 miles (8 kilometers) above sea level
– highest of all clouds
– look white, curly, feathery, delicate, streaky, wispy, thin
– sometimes called "mares' tails" because they tend to look like the tails of horses
– move at speeds of 100 to 200 miles per hour, but their height makes their speed seem much slower
– made entirely of ice crystals because it is so cold at that altitude

Stratus Clouds

– found 2 to 4 miles (3–6 kilometers) above the Earth
– middle range in height from Earth
– usually arranged in smooth, flat layers
– look like a gray sheet or blanket, but not very thick, so blue sky often shines through
– sometimes called "mackerel sky" in English because they look like the scales of a fish (called *mouton* for "sheep" in French)
– often signal that bad weather may be coming
– made of water droplets

Cumulus Clouds

– found about 1 mile (1.6 kilometers) high
– their base is closest to Earth of all clouds, but their tops may rise to great heights, making them look like rising towers
– detached, look like cauliflowers
– large masses of clouds, fluffy and dome-shaped with a flat, gray base
– usually seen in summer
– if they become too dense and vertical, they often produce heavy rain, lightning, and thunder
– sometimes called "thunderheads"
– tornadoes come from thunderheads
– made of water droplets

A. Draft your three supporting paragraphs on a separate piece of paper.

B. Exchange papers with a classmate. Discuss any suggestions that your partner has for revising and editing. Then copy your article onto another sheet of paper. Include the introduction and add a short conclusion.

Writing a Classification Essay

In this activity you will practice writing an essay that classifies a topic into several categories. Follow these steps:

a. Prewriting
Choose one of the following topics and do a prewriting activity such as clustering, freewriting, or brainstorming to generate some ideas about how to classify it. Use the space on the next page.

    1. Types of mistakes people make when learning a second language
    2. Types of students
    3. Types of martial arts
    4. Kinds of vices

(continued on next page)

5. Kinds of engineers (or doctors, lawyers)
6. Types of athletes
7. Your choice

b. Planning

Using the ideas you generated in your prewriting, determine the most appropriate method of classification. Make sure your categories are mutually exclusive. Then prepare an informal outline of your essay.

c. Drafting

On a separate piece of paper, write the first draft of your essay. Refer to the essay plan on page 82 to help you write your draft. Be sure to provide some background information in the introduction and include a clear thesis statement. Organize the body of the essay so that you discuss one category in each supporting paragraph. End with a conclusion that restates the method of classification and summarizes the categories.

d. Personal Revising

Put your essay away for at least one day before you begin to revise it. Then use the checklist on page 54 to revise the first draft. Be sure that all your paragraphs are unified and coherent. Also, check to make sure you have provided enough support to prove the main idea of each paragraph. Write or type a revised version of your essay.

e. Peer Revising

Exchange drafts with a classmate for more suggestions on revision. Use the following questions to help you improve your partner's essay:

1. What technique did the author use in the introduction?
2. Was the technique effective? If not, how do you think the introduction could be improved?
3. Are the categories used in the classification mutually exclusive? If not, can you think of another way to classify the topic?
4. Did the author give an adequate description of each category? If not, where is more information needed?
5. What are the strengths and weaknesses of the conclusion?

Incorporate any suggestions your partner has made that you agree with.

f. Editing

Use the checklist on page 65 to edit your essay. Correct all the grammar, punctuation, capitalization, and spelling errors before you copy it over or type it.

(You) Be the Editor

The following classification paragraph describes the three types of consumer products. The content of the paragraph is correct, but there are nine mistakes. Find the mistakes and correct them. Then copy the corrected paragraph on a separate piece of paper.

Consumer products are usually divided into three categories, convenience, shopping, and specialty products. Each category is based on the way people buys products. Convenience products are products that a consumer needs but that he or she is not willing to spend very much time or effort shopping for. Convenience products usually inexpensive, frequently purchased items. Some common examples are bread, newspapers soda, and gasoline. Buyers spend few time planning the purchase of a convenience product. Also do not compare brands or sellers. The second category, shopping products, are those products that customers feel are worth the time and effort to compare with competing products. Furniture, refrigerators, cars, and televisions are examples of shopping products. Because these products are expected to last a long time. They are purchased less frequently than convenience products. The last category is specialty products. Specialty products are consumer products that the customer really wants and makes a special effort to find and buying. Buyers actually plan the purchase of a specialty product. They know what they want and will not accept a substitute. Fancy photographic equipment and a haircut by a certain stylist are examples of specialty products. In searching for specialty products. Buyers do not compare alternatives.

On Your Own

Choose one of the following topics and write a classification essay. Make sure that your introduction gives the method of classification, identifies the categories, and states the purpose. Also, make sure that your categories are mutually exclusive.

1. Types of magazines
2. Styles of architecture
3. Kinds of phobias

Cause/Effect

When the purpose of your essay is to analyze the causes (reasons) or effects (results) of a situation, you will use a **cause/effect pattern of organization**. When you are answering questions such as, "Why did you decide to major in physics?" or "What effects will learning English have on your career?" you are analyzing a situation according to its causes or effects.

In academic writing, you will frequently need to use the cause/effect pattern of organization. For example, in a psychology class, you might need to discuss the effects of hypnosis on patients with chronic pain or the reasons why hypnosis is recommended for some people. In a history class, you might be asked to analyze the technological causes of the industrial revolution or the effects of the industrial revolution on family life in England. In an economics class, you might be required to explain the reasons for the high inflation rate in Brazil or the effects of the high rate of inflation on the Brazilian middle class. In an anthropology course, you might need to explore the reasons why many of the world's languages are disappearing or the effects of their disappearance on indigenous populations.

The Language of Cause and Effect: Useful Expressions and Sentence Patterns		
Study the following transition signals that indicate a cause-effect relationship:		
as a result	since	because
due to	therefore	consequently
thus	then	as a consequence
for this reason	so	and that is why

The following sentence patterns are useful in writing topic sentences and thesis statements for cause-and-effect paragraphs and essays.

1. **There are several** | causes of
reasons for _____.
effects of

There are several causes of jet lag.

2. **There are** | three
four **main reasons why** _____.
several

There are three ***main reasons why*** I want to get my own apartment.

3. _____ **has had** | several
many **important effects on** _____.
a few

My parents' divorce **has had** *several* **important effects on** *my life.*

Write a thesis statement for each of the following essay topics. Use a variety of sentence patterns.

1. Topic: The effects of unemployment

   Thesis statement: _____

   _____

2. Topic: The causes of depletion of the ozone layer

   Thesis statement: _____

   _____

3. Topic: The reasons you decided to learn English

   Thesis statement: _____

   _____

4. Topic: The effects of forest fires

   Thesis statement: _____

   _____

5. Topic: The effects of culture shock

   Thesis statement: _____

   _____

Describing Causes and Effects

Look at the news photographs on pages 88 and 89 and write sentences of cause and effect. Use a variety of expressions.

EXAMPLE:

   a. Many fish and water birds died because of the oil spill.
   b. Due to the oil spill, sea life in this area has been devastated.
   c. As a result of the oil spill, thousands of dead lobsters have washed up on the beach.

1.

a. _____

b. _____

c. _____

2.

a. _____

b. _____

c. _____

3.

a. _____

b. _____

c. _____

4.

a. _____

b. _____

c. _____

Writing a Paragraph of Causes

Read the following conversation between two friends.

MARK: Hi, Janie. How long have you been here?

JANIE: It seems like hours, but I actually didn't get here until 9:30. The lines are so long, and half the courses I wanted are already closed.

MARK: I'll bet you wish you'd preregistered.

JANIE: I sure do, but I was planning to change my major and I didn't know what courses I'd need this semester.

MARK: So, you've decided not to go into anthropology after all? What happened?

JANIE: I realized the job prospects weren't too good for an anthropologist with only a B.A. degree.

MARK: What about graduate school?

JANIE: I thought about that, but I really want to start working right after graduation. Maybe I'll go to grad school in a few years, but for now I want something more practical.

(continued on next page)

MARK: I can relate to that. That's why I'm majoring in engineering. Anyway, what department are you switching to?

JANIE: Believe it or not, I've decided to go into nursing.

MARK: That's great, but it'll be a big change after anthro.

JANIE: I know, but I've always liked working with people and helping others. When I was in high school, I did a lot of volunteer work at the local hospital.

Mark: Well, good luck with your new career. I guess we won't be in any of the same classes this semester.

Using information from the conversation, write a paragraph that describes the reasons Janie is changing her major. Be sure to include a topic sentence and transitions.

_____

_____

_____

_____

_____

_____

_____

Analyzing a Cause/Effect Essay

Read the essay and answer the questions that follow.

The Extinction of the Dinosaurs

For almost 140 million years, dinosaurs and other large reptiles ruled the land, sky, and sea. Dinosaurs came in sizes and shapes suited to every corner of the world. Then, approximately 65 million years ago, these huge reptiles died out and mammals took over the Earth. Few mysteries have ever excited the imaginations of scientists as much as this great extinction that killed off all the dinosaurs. Over the years, scientists have developed many theories to explain the disappearance of the dinosaurs and the other great reptiles. Three of the most common explanations are a gradual change in the Earth's climate, a lack of food, and the Earth's collision with a large asteroid.

Traditionally, scientists believed that the number of dinosaurs declined slowly for millions of years before they eventually disappeared. Many studies of fossils point to a slow change in the environmental conditions on Earth. This led to a generally cooler climate. Toward the end of the Cretaceous Period, the climate may have become too cold for the dinosaurs. Many dinosaurs were too big to hibernate in dens. In addition, they lacked fur or feathers for protection against the cold. Smaller animals had the advantage of being able to hibernate during cold periods. Mammals and birds were better suited to withstand the cold because they had fur or feathers for protection. It may have been easier for these animals to migrate to warmer places to avoid the cold weather. In these ways, such animals could have survived the colder climate that may have slowly killed off the dinosaurs.

Another explanation of dinosaur extinction has to do with food. Some experts think that plant-eating dinosaurs could not digest the new kinds of plants that developed during the Cretaceous Period. Eventually, they starved to death. As the plant-eating dinosaurs died off, so did the meat-eaters who fed on them. Other experts believe that since the dinosaurs could not compete successfully with mammals for food, they eventually lost the struggle for existence.

Today, some scientists believe that the cause of the extinction was much more sudden and catastrophic. In the late 1970s, scientists discovered evidence for the abrupt end to the Age of Dinosaurs. Dr. Louis Alvarez and his colleagues arrived at a revolutionary hypothesis to explain the extinction of dinosaurs. They suggest that about 65 million years ago, the Earth was struck by a huge asteroid. The asteroid was destroyed in the explosion and billions of tons of dust were thrown up into the air. A thick cloud of dust blocked out sunlight for a long time. Without the sun's energy, plants were not able to make food and they died. The lack of plants killed off many of the plant-eating dinosaurs, which then caused the death of the meat-eating dinosaurs that preyed on them. The darkness caused temperatures to fall below freezing for many months. This sudden change in climate further decreased the dinosaur populations.

It seems that no one theory adequately explains why dinosaurs died out. Perhaps dinosaurs simply could not adjust to the changes that were taking place on the Earth toward the end of the Cretaceous Period. Most likely, it was a combination of causes that contributed to the end of the Age of Dinosaurs.

Pair Work

Answer the following questions with a partner:

1. What three main causes does the author suggest to explain the extinction of the dinosaurs?
2. How are the supporting paragraphs organized?
3. What techniques are used in the introduction and conclusion?
4. What transitions did the author use to achieve coherence? Underline them in the essay.

Essay Plan: Cause/Effect

The guidelines below will help you remember what you need to do in each part of a cause or effect essay.

Introduction

1. Provide background information about the situation you are analyzing.
2. Describe the situation.
3. Identify its main causes or effects.

Supporting Paragraphs

1. Explain one cause or effect in each supporting paragraph.
2. If there are many causes or effects, group them into several main categories.
3. Organize the causes or effects, using time order or order of importance.

Conclusion

1. Summarize the main causes or effects.
2. Draw a conclusion or make a prediction.

Ready to Write

Writing an Essay of Causes

You are a reporter for a health magazine. Your assignment is to write an article on the topic of *the causes of heart disease*. You have just conducted an interview with a cardiologist, Dr. Harvey Snyder, and have written the following introduction:

> Heart disease affects so many people that it has become a serious concern for medical science. The heart is a complex organ that is vulnerable to hereditary as well as environmental risks. Cardiologists think of these risk factors as major and minor causes.

Dr. Snyder has identified a number of risk factors associated with heart disease. He has grouped these risk factors into major and minor causes. Here are your notes from the interview:

Major causes of heart disease:

1. *Family history—you are at a higher risk for developing heart disease if your parents or grandparents have had it.*

2. *High blood pressure—causes the heart to work too hard and can damage arteries.*

3. *High cholesterol levels—dangerous because fatty deposits build up in blood vessels.*

4. *Diabetes—can lead to hardening of the arteries and heart attacks.*

5. *Smoking cigarettes—smokers are two or three times more likely to have a heart attack than nonsmokers.*

Minor causes of heart disease:

1. *Having a Type A personality—becoming easily stressed, being overly competitive, aggressive, and intense.*

2. *Having a sedentary lifestyle— not getting enough exercise.*

3. *Obesity—being extremely overweight and having a poor diet.*

A. On a separate piece of paper, write a draft of your two supporting paragraphs in which you discuss the major and minor causes of heart disease.

B. Exchange papers with a classmate. Discuss any suggestions that your partner has for revision and editing.

C. Write a conclusion for your article. Suggest ways to beat the risks of heart disease by adopting a healthful lifestyle and good personal habits.

D. Copy your entire article, including the introduction, body, and conclusion, onto another sheet of paper.

WRITING AN ESSAY OF EFFECTS

In this activity you will practice writing an essay that analyzes the effects of a situation. Follow these steps:

a. Prewriting

Choose one of the following topics and do a prewriting activity such as clustering, freewriting, or brainstorming to generate some ideas about its effects.

1. The effects of divorce on family life
2. The effects of a natural disaster such as an earthquake or hurricane
3. The effects of climate on lifestyle
4. The effects of a social, political, or economic problem in a country you are familiar with
5. The effects that your peers have had on you

b. Planning

Using the ideas you generated in your prewriting, identify several major effects and prepare an informal outline of your essay.

c. Drafting

On a separate piece of paper, write the first draft of your essay. Use the essay plan on page 91 to help you organize your draft. Be sure to provide some background information about your topic in the introduction and include a clear thesis statement that states its main effects. Organize the body paragraphs according to order of importance, with the most important effect last. End with a conclusion that summarizes the main effects, draws a conclusion, or makes a prediction.

d. Personal Revising

Wait at least one day and then revise your essay using the checklist on page 54. Be sure all your paragraphs are unified and coherent. Also, check to make sure that you have provided enough support to fully describe each effect. Write or type a revised version of your essay.

e. Peer Revising

Exchange drafts with a classmate for further suggestions for improvement. Read your partner's essay and think about its strengths and weaknesses. The following suggestions will help you:

1. Does the introduction provide enough background information to get you interested in the topic? If it does not, offer some suggestions on how to improve it.
2. Check for the effectiveness of the overall organization of the essay. Make sure that the paragraphs are arranged in a logical order. If they are not, help your partner rearrange them.
3. Evaluate the body paragraphs for support, coherence, and unity. If you notice any problems, suggest some specific ways to revise the paragraphs.
4. Review the conclusion and offer some suggestions for improvement if needed.

Incorporate any suggestions your partner has made that you agree with.

f. Editing

Use the checklist on page 65 to edit your essay. Correct all the grammar, punctuation, capitalization, and spelling errors before you copy it over or type it.

You Be the Editor

The paragraph that follows discusses the effects of the Great Depression. The content of the paragraph is correct, but there are eleven mistakes. Find the mistakes and correct them. Then copy the corrected paragraph on a separate piece of paper.

The Great Depression of the 1930s affected Americans for generations. The complete collapse of the stock market began on October 24 1929, when 13 million shares of stock were sold. On Tuesday, October 29, known as Black Tuesday, more than 16 million shares were sold. The value of most shares fell sharply, resulting in financial ruin and widespread panic. Although there have been other financial panics. None has had such a devastating and long-term effect as the Great Depression. By 1932, the industrial output of the united states had been cut in half. One-fourth of the labor force, about 15 million people, was out of work, and hourly wages dropped almost 50 percent. In addition, hundreds of banks will fail. Prices for agricultural products dropped to their lowest level since the Civil War. More than 90,000 businesses failed complete. Statistics, however, cannot tell the story of the extraordinary hardships the masses of americans suffered. For nearly every unemployed people, there were dependents who needed to be fed and housed. People in the United States had never known such massive poverty and hunger before. Former millionaires stood on street corners trying to selling apples at 5 cents apiece. Thousands lose their homes. Because they could not pay their mortgages. Some people moved in with relatives. Others moved to shabby sections of town and built shelters out of tin cans and cardboard. Homeless people slept outside under old newspapers. Many Americans waited in lines in every city, hoping for something to eat. Unfortunately, many of these people died of malnutrition. In 1931 alone, more than 20,000 Americans committed suicide.

On Your Own

Choose one of the following general subjects and brainstorm a list of its causes or effects. Using the ideas generated from your list, write an essay of causes or effects.

1. Water or air pollution
2. Unemployment
3. War
4. An important historical event in your country

Comparison/ Contrast

Very often in your writing, you will want to show how ideas, people, or things are similar or different. When you **compare** two things, you look for how they are similar. When you **contrast** two things, you look for how they are different. It is important that the two things you compare or contrast belong to the same general class. For example, you probably would not want to compare or contrast a house and a dog. You could, however, compare and contrast a Japanese house and a North American house.

In academic writing, comparison and contrast are often used to support a point or persuade the reader. For example, in a political science class, you might compare and contrast two leaders to show which one was more successful at bringing about economic reforms. In a literature class, you might compare and contrast two short stories to show which one you liked better. In an engineering class, you might compare and contrast two methods of combustion to show which one is more efficient.

The Language of Comparison and Contrast:
Useful Phrases and Sentence Patterns

The following signals indicate a comparison:

in the same way that	similarly	compared to
both	is similar to	is like
have in common	just as	likewise

The following signals indicate a contrast:

however	nevertheless	unlike
although	on the other hand	whereas
even though	in spite of	while
but	on the contrary	is different from
yet	still	differs from
in contrast	conversely	

The following sentence patterns are useful in writing topic sentences and thesis statements for comparison/contrast essays and paragraphs:

1. **There are several** | differences **between** _____ **and** _____.
   | similarities

   There are several *differences **between** high school **and** college.*

2. _____ **and** _____ **are** | similar **in many ways.**
   | different

   *Thai food **and** Vietnamese food **are** similar **in many ways.***

3. _____ **is** | different from _____ **in many ways.**
   | similar to

   *My father **is** different from his older brother **in many ways.***

4. _____ **and** _____ **have** | several **things in common.**
   | many

   *My best friend **and** I **have** several **things in common.***

5. **A comparison between** _____ **and** _____ | reveals _____.
   | shows
   | demonstrates

   A comparison between *jazz **and** rock 'n' roll reveals some surprising similarities.*

Write a thesis statement for a comparison/contrast essay on each of the following topics. Use a variety of sentence patterns.

1. Topic: Your two best friends

   Thesis statement: _____

   _____

2. Topic: Soccer and rugby

   Thesis statement: _____

   _____

3. Topic: Capitalism and communism

   Thesis statement: _____

   _____

4. Topic: American cars and Japanese cars

   Thesis statement: _____

   _____

5. Topic: Two of your classmates

   Thesis statement: _____

   _____

Examining Comparisons and Contrasts

Look at the following two classified ads for apartments for rent. Find several similarities and differences between the two apartments. Write two sentences of comparison and two sentences of contrast. Use a variety of sentence patterns.

Apartments for Rent

Large 2-bedroom apt., 2 bathrooms, eat-in kitchen, large living room, air-conditioning, wall-to-wall carpeting, great location on Monument Street, NO pets, $700/month, all utilities included. Call Mr. Toll at (315) 446-3377.

Apartments for Rent

Huron Towers: 10th floor—great view of river. 3 bedrooms, 2 bathrooms, modern kitchen with new appliances, fireplace in living room, hardwood floors, air-conditioning, laundry facilities, utilities NOT included. NO pets. Pool and tennis courts on premises. $995/month. Call for appointment: (315) 885-3909.

EXAMPLE

The apartment on Monument Street has fewer bedrooms than the apartment in Huron Towers.

a. _____

b. _____

c. _____

d. _____

Now do the same for the next two sets of classified ads.

Used Cars For Sale

1996 Toyota Camry. Automatic transmission. Excellent condition. Fully loaded. 18,000 miles. Gray leather interior, dark green exterior. ABS brakes. Sun roof. Driver's side air bag. CD player. $21,000.

Used Cars For Sale

1995 Audi Quattro. Mint condition. Standard transmission. 25,000 miles. Loaded. Silver with black leather interior. Sun roof. ABS brakes. Seat heaters. Tape deck. Dual air bags. Theft alarm system. $28,000.

a. _____

b. _____

c. _____

d. _____

Pets

Golden Retriever puppy for sale. 5-month-old male. Championship stock. Great with kids. One-year health guarantee. $350. Call (617) 368-3254.

Pets

German Shepherd puppy needs home. Female, 7 months. House-trained. Excellent watch dog. Health guarantee. Top quality. $400. Call (617) 576-3124 after 6PM.

a. _____

b. _____

c. _____

d. _____

Writing a Comparison Paragraph

You are studying the impact of heredity on human behavior and are doing research on identical twins who were separated at birth. The paragraph below is the introductory paragraph you have written for your report:

> Some of the most important research in the field of behavioral genetics comes from the studies of identical twins who were separated at birth. Dr. Thomas J. Bouchard is a professor at the University of Minnesota who has conducted many influential studies on identical twins. He believes that by examining their differences and similarities, we will better understand the mysteries of heredity and environment. One of the most revealing pair of twins that Dr. Bouchard has studied is known as "the Jim twins." Jim Springer and Jim Lewis are identical twins who were separated at birth because their 14-year-old mother could not take care of them. They were not reunited until 39 years later. According to Dr. Bouchard, the Jim twins are "the most valuable pair that has ever been studied" because they were separated for so long and because the similarities between them are so astounding.
>
> Source: *Good Housekeeping*, February 1980

Now write the paragraph on the similarities between Jim Springer and Jim Lewis. The following is a list of the similarities that you have gathered. There are too many similarities listed here for one paragraph. Choose the ones that you think are the most interesting to include in your paragraph. Remember to begin your paragraph with a clearly stated topic sentence.

- Each brother was told that his brother had died at birth.
- Both brothers are emotional, sentimental, kind, generous, friendly, and loving by nature.
- Neither brother is prone to anger and if he does get angry, he doesn't show it.
- Both bite their fingernails and/or jiggle one foot when nervous.
- Both smoke Salem cigarettes.
- Both drink Miller Lite beer.
- They look exactly alike in terms of facial features.
- They are both 6 feet tall and weigh 180 pounds.
- They walk the same way.
- Both cross their legs the same way.
- Their voices sound exactly the same.
- They use the same gestures when they speak.
- Both use the same expressions such as "Mama mía" and "Cool."
- Both enjoy woodworking and have built several birdhouses and tables.
- Both brothers are poor spellers.
- Both were married first to women named Linda.
- Their second wives were both named Betty.
- As children, they each had a dog and named it Toy.
- They have both taken family vacations on the same beach in Florida.
- Until they were reunited, each had felt an emptiness, as though something was missing from his life.
- Jim Springer named his son James Allen; Jim Lewis named his son James Alan.
- Both frequently buy gifts (that they cannot afford) for their wives.
- Both men have worked part-time in law enforcement.

Now revise and edit your paragraph. Copy it over and give it to your teacher.

Methods of Organization for Comparison and Contrast

There are two basic patterns for writing a comparison/contrast essay: the **block method** and the **point-by-point method.**

In the block method, you describe all the similarities in the first body paragraph and then all the differences in the second body paragraph.

In the point-by-point method, you identify several important points to be compared and contrasted. In the first body paragraph, you compare and contrast the two things according to the first point. In the second body paragraph, you compare and contrast the two things according to the second point, and so on.

Most student writers find the block method easier to master.

Analyzing Essays of Comparison and Contrast

Read the following two essays and answer the questions. The purpose of both essays is to explain why a student chose to attend Greenwell University rather than State University.

Essay 1

Last week when I received acceptances from my top two choices for college, State and Greenwell, I knew I had a difficult decision to make. Although I had talked to friends and relatives who had attended both schools and had visited both campuses many times, I couldn't make up my mind. It was only after I analyzed the similarities and differences between the two schools that I finally came to my decision to begin classes at Greenwell in the fall.

At first glance, it seems that State and Greenwell have a lot in common. First of all, both universities are located in Pennsylvania, where I am from. The tuition is also exactly the same at both schools—$20,000 per year. In addition, the basketball team at State is just as good as the one at Greenwell, and I would love to play for either one. Most importantly, both schools have large libraries, excellent academic reputations, and first-class engineering departments.

It was when I looked at the differences between the two schools that I made my final decision. In terms of location, State is more attractive. Its setting in a safe suburb was definitely more appealing than Greenwell's location in a dangerous city neighborhood. I also liked State's older campus with its beautiful buildings and trees more than Greenwell's new campus, which looks like an office complex. But I realized that these should not be the most important factors in my decision. I had to pay a lot of attention to the financial component. Although the tuition is the same at both schools, Greenwell offered me a $3,000 scholarship, whereas State couldn't give me any financial aid. In addition, if I go to Greenwell, I can live at home and save money on room and board. Since Greenwell is much closer to home, I won't have to spend as much on transportation home during vacation breaks. The most important factor in making my decision was the difference in class size between the two universities. State has large classes and an impersonal feeling. On the other hand, Greenwell has small classes, and students get a lot of personal attention.

In conclusion, after taking everything into consideration, I think I made the right decision. Since small classes, personal attention from my professors, and saving money are all very important to me, I will probably be happier at Greenwell.

Pair Work

Answer the following questions with a partner:

1. What method did the author of this essay use?

   _____

2. What is the thesis statement?

   _____

3. What is the topic sentence of the first body paragraph?

   _____

4. What similarities between the two schools does the author mention?

   _____

   _____

   _____

   _____

5. What is the topic sentence of the second body paragraph?

   _____

6. What differences between the two schools does the author mention?

   _____

   _____

   _____

   _____

Essay 2

Last week when I received acceptances from my top two choices for college, State and Greenwell, I knew I had a difficult decision to make. Although I had talked to friends and relatives who had attended both schools and I had visited both campuses many times, I couldn't make up my mind. It was only after I compared the location, cost, and quality of education of the two schools that I could finally come to my decision to attend Greenwell.

The first thing I considered was the location. First of all, both universities are located in Pennsylvania, where I am from. But that is where the similarities end. State's setting in a safe suburb is definitely more appealing than Greenwell's location in a dangerous city neighborhood. I also like State's older campus with its beautiful buildings and gardens more than Greenwell's new campus, which looks like an office complex.

(continued on next page)

In addition to location, I had to pay a lot of attention to the financial component. The tuition is the same at both schools—$20,000 per year. However, Greenwell offered me a $3,000 scholarship, but State couldn't give me any money. Also, if I go to Greenwell, I can live at home and save money on room and board. Finally, since Greenwell is much closer to home, I won't have to spend as much on transportation home during vacation breaks.

The quality of education at the two schools had the most influence on my decision. In many ways, State and Greenwell have similar standards of education. Both schools have large libraries and excellent academic reputations. Also, State has a first-class engineering department, and so does Greenwell. So I had to look at other things. What it came down to was the difference in class size between the two universities. State has large classes and an impersonal feeling. On the other hand, Greenwell has small classes, and students get a lot of personal attention.

In conclusion, after taking everything into consideration, I think I made the right decision. Since small classes and personal attention from my professors are very important to me, I will probably be happier at Greenwell.

Pair Work

Answer the following questions with a partner:

1. What method did the author of this essay use?

   _____

2. What is the thesis statement?

   _____

3. What three points about the schools did the author compare and contrast?

   _____

   _____

   _____

4. How did the author organize the order of the supporting paragraphs?

   _____

5. What transitions did the author use to achieve coherence? Underline them in the essay.

Essay Plans: Comparison/Contrast

Block Method
The guidelines below will help you remember what you need to do in each part of a comparison/contrast essay using the block method.

Introduction

1. Provide background information about your topic.
2. Identify the two things being compared and contrasted.
3. State the purpose for making the comparison and/or contrast.

Supporting Paragraphs

1. In the first paragraph(s), discuss the similarities.
2. In the next paragraph(s), discuss the differences.

Conclusion

1. Restate the purpose for comparison and/or contrast in different words.
2. Summarize the main similarities and differences.
3. Draw a conclusion.

Point-by-Point Method
The guidelines below will help you remember what you need to do in each section of a comparison/contrast essay using the point-by-point method.

Introduction

1. Provide background information about your topic.
2. Identify the two things being compared and contrasted.
3. State the purpose for making the comparison and/or contrast.
4. Identify the points to be compared and contrasted.

Supporting Paragraphs

1. In the first paragraph, compare and/or contrast the two things according to the first point.
2. In the second paragraph, compare and/or contrast the two things according to the second point.
3. In the third and subsequent paragraphs, do the same thing.

Conclusion

1. Restate the purpose for comparison and/or contrast in different words.
2. Summarize the main similarities and differences.
3. Draw a conclusion.

Writing an Essay of Comparison and Contrast: Block Method

In this activity, you will practice writing an essay of comparison and contrast. Follow these steps:

a. Prewriting
Choose one of the following topics and use the space on the next page to brainstorm a list of similarities and differences.

1. Compare and contrast yourself and another member of your family.
2. Compare and contrast some aspect of your culture, such as eating habits, education, government, economy, religion, or social life, with the same aspect of another culture.
3. Compare and contrast two works of art on the same subject but in different media, such as a poem and a photograph, or a painting and a song.
4. Compare and contrast two people you have worked with, such as two co-workers at a job, two students in a group, two secretaries you have known, or two bosses you have had.

b. Planning

Organize your list by grouping the similarities in one group and the differences in another group. Then prepare an informal outline for you essay. Be sure that you have identified a purpose for making your comparison. For example, are you comparing two restaurants so that you can recommend one of them to a friend? Are you comparing your native language and English to show why English is easy or difficult for you to learn? How you develop your essay will depend on your purpose.

c. Drafting

On a separate piece of paper, write the first draft of your essay. Refer to the essay plan on page 103 to help you write your draft. Be sure to provide some background information in the introduction and include a clear thesis statement that states your purpose for comparison. Organize the body paragraphs so that all the similarities are in one paragraph and all the differences are in another paragraph. End with a conclusion that restates your purpose for the comparison and that summarizes the main similarities and differences.

d. Personal Revising

Put your essay away for at least one day. Use the checklist on page 54 to revise the first draft. Be sure that all your paragraphs are unified and coherent. Also, check to make sure you have provided enough support to explain fully the similarities and differences. Write or type a revised version of your essay.

e. Peer Revising

Exchange drafts with a classmate for suggestions on how to improve your essays. Use the following questions as a guide:

1. Did the introduction identify the two items being compared?
2. Is the purpose of the comparison clearly stated?
3. Did the introduction make you want to read the rest of the essay? Why or why not?
4. Did the author adequately develop the points of comparison in a unified paragraph? If not, offer suggestions for strengthening the paragraph.
5. Did the author adequately develop the points of contrast in another unified paragraph? If not, offer suggestions for strengthening the paragraph.
6. Did the author include an effective conclusion?

Incorporate any suggestions your partner has made that you agree with.

f. Editing

Use the checklist on page 65 to edit your essay. Correct all the grammar, punctuation, capitalization, and spelling errors before you copy it over or type it.

You Be the Editor

The following paragraph contains nine mistakes. Find the mistakes and correct them. Then, copy the corrected paragraph onto a separate sheet of paper.

Now that I am pregnant with our first child, my husband and I will have to find a bigger place to live. Our little apartment in the city is too small for three people. We trying to decide whether we should get a biggest apartment in the city or move to the suburbs. We have four main considerations expense, space, convenience, and schools. In general, is probably expensiver to live in the city. On the other hand, we would have to buy a car if we moved to the suburbs we would also have to buy a lawnmower and a snowblower or hire someone care for the lawn and driveway. In terms of space, we could definitely have a bigger house and much more land if we lived in the suburbs. However, we wonder if it would be worth it, since we would lose so many conveniences. Stores would be farther away and so would friends, neighbors, movie theaters, museums, and restaurants. The most biggest inconvenience would be that we would both have to commute to work every day instead of walking or taking the bus. The Schools are probably better in the suburbs, but for our child, who isn't even born yet, school is several years away. In looking at our priorities, it becomes clear that we should continue to live in the city for now and then reevaluate our decision as the baby gets closer to school age.

On Your Own

This time, you will write a comparison/contrast essay using the point-by-point method. Choose one of the topics below and identify several points on which to base your comparison. Follow the five steps of good writing as you write your essay, and be sure that you have a clear purpose for your comparison.

1. Compare and contrast two items such as a computer and a typewriter, glasses and contact lenses, or a compact disc and a cassette tape.
2. Compare and contrast dating customs in your generation and your grandparents' generation.

Problem/Solution

CHAPTER 9

When your purpose is to describe a problem and evaluate possible solutions, use a **problem/solution pattern of organization.** For example, if you are discussing solutions to the problem of employee dissatisfaction in your company or the problems of adjusting to a foreign culture, you would use this type of organization. You should organize your solutions according to order of importance.

The problem/solution pattern is very useful in academic writing. For example, you would use it in a sociology class if you were asked to describe the problem of overpopulation and offer several solutions. You could also use this pattern in an economics class if you needed to analyze the problem of unemployment and suggest some ways to solve it.

Examining Solutions

For each of the problems described below, think of at least three possible solutions. Work in small groups and then compare your solutions with those of your classmates.

1. Living in a foreign country can be fun and exciting, but it can also be problematic. One of the most serious problems that people living in a foreign country face is culture shock. What ways can you think of to help people deal with this problem?

   PROBLEM: Culture shock

   SOLUTIONS: a. _____

   b. _____

   c. _____

2. Many people have trouble falling asleep or staying asleep for an adequate amount of time. This problem is known as insomnia. What suggestions would you give to people who cannot seem to get a good night's sleep?

   PROBLEM: Insomnia

   SOLUTIONS: a. _____

   b. _____

   c. _____

3. Stress at work or school can be a serious problem. A person suffering from too much stress usually finds it difficult to be productive or happy. What are some ways to reduce the amount of stress in someone's life?

PROBLEM: Stress at work or school

SOLUTIONS: a. _____

               b. _____

               c. _____

4. The population of the world keeps growing. Every 15 seconds, approximately 100 babies are born. Experts predict that by the year 2000, there could be 6 billion people on our planet. By the end of the next century, the population could reach 10 billion people. The problem is that there probably won't be enough food to feed everyone. What solutions can you come up with to help solve this problem?

PROBLEM: Overpopulation

SOLUTIONS: a. _____

               b. _____

               c. _____

5. Crime is a serious problem in many large cities. Look back at the introduction to an essay on crime on page 43. Is crime a serious problem in the large cities in your native country? What solutions can you think of to reduce the amount of crime?

PROBLEM: Crime in large cities in the United States (or another country)

SOLUTIONS: a. _____

               b. _____

               c. _____

6. Illiteracy is a serious problem all over the world. For example, one-third of adult Americans are functionally illiterate. People who cannot read and write have many disadvantages functioning in society. What solutions can you come up with to help overcome this problem?

PROBLEM: Illiteracy

SOLUTIONS: a. _____

               b. _____

               c. _____

7. Many of the Earth's resources are nonrenewable and will eventually run out. In order to make our valuable natural resources last longer, we need to conserve materials and recycle them as much as possible. Unfortunately, it is not always easy to convince people of the necessity of recycling. What ideas do you have about getting people to recycle?

PROBLEM: Getting people to recycle

SOLUTIONS: a. _____

               b. _____

               c. _____

Practicing Solutions

You are the advice consultant for a newspaper. How would you respond to the following letters? Be sure to offer several solutions to each problem in your response. Share your responses by exchanging papers with your classmates or by reading them out loud.

Dear Advisor,

When I first came to the United States to study Western literature, I never dreamed I would fall in love—especially with an American. I had planned to spend two years here getting my master's degree and then return to Japan and teach. Now, only nine months later, everything has changed. I met Jim in one of my classes, and we started studying together. One thing led to the next and before I knew it, I was engaged. It wasn't exactly love at first sight, but almost. Jim's parents are wonderful. They say that they would love to have a Japanese daughter-in-law. Unfortunately, my parents are a different story. They can't accept the fact that I would marry someone who isn't Japanese. They are very upset and want me to forget about Jim and all our plans for a wedding when we graduate. In fact, they are urging me to come home at the end of the semester and spend the summer in Japan. They think that I'll get over Jim if I don't see him for three months. I'm so confused. I am really close to my parents and don't want to hurt them. On the other hand, I love Jim and want to spend the rest of my life with him. I think I would be happy living in the United States, but I'm afraid my parents would never get over it. What suggestions do you have for me? HELP!!

Confused

Dear Confused,

_____

_____

_____

_____

_____

Dear Advisor,

    I am a sophomore in college. Last year my roommate, Fred, and I were very good friends. I don't know what happened, but this year everything has changed. Fred seems really different. He has a whole new group of friends and spends all of his time with them. He stays out late at night and often doesn't get up in time for his classes. He never studies any more and he got kicked off the wrestling team for missing so many practices. He is always either sleeping or out with his new friends. When he is in our room, he is moody, messy, and undependable. Please tell me what to do. I've tried talking to him, but he just tells me to mind my own business. I'm concerned that he is going to get kicked out of school. He is already on academic probation. What should I do?

                           A Concerned Roommate

Dear Concerned,

_____

_____

_____

_____

_____

On Your Own

Write your own letter to the advice consultant. You can write about a real problem that you have or make one up. Then, exchange letters with a classmate and write a response.

Writing a Problem/Solution Paragraph

CASE STUDY

You are taking an introductory business course. You have been asked to analyze the following case. Read the case and study the drawings of Restaurant Row and the Undergrad Grill. Pay attention to the menu and the sign on the door of the Undergrad Grill.

UNDERGRAD GRILL

NO Bare feet
NO Smoking
NO Skateboards
NO Children
    under Age 5
NO take out

UNDERGRAD GRILL

Open 11 A.M. to 11 P.M.

Soups

Hot and sour	$ 4.00
Black bean	$ 4.00
French onion	$ 4.00
Wonton	$ 4.00
Vegetable	$ 4.00

Entrées

Hamburger	$ 8.95
Cheeseburger	$10.95
Fried chicken	$ 9.95
Filet of fish	$ 6.95
Chicken fajita	$ 8.95
Beef fajita	$10.95
Shrimp tempura	$10.95
Pork fried rice	$ 6.95
Steak au poivre	$12.95
Spaghetti and meatballs	$ 7.95
Chicken and hummus	$ 8.95
Lamb curry	$14.95

Vegetables & Side Dishes

Baked potato	$ 3.00
French fries	$ 3.00
Rice	$ 3.00
Corn on the cob (in season)	$ 3.00
Peas	$ 3.00
Green beans	$ 3.00
House salad	$ 4.50

Desserts

Homemade apple pie	$ 5.00
Chocolate mousse	$ 5.00
Flan	$ 5.00
Ice cream	$ 4.00
Mixed fresh fruit	$ 3.50

Drinks

Lemonade	$ 4.00
Coffee	$ 3.00
Tea	$ 3.00
Soda	$ 2.00

Credit cards accepted. No checks.

Business Case #22

On April 15, Tom Higgins opened a new restaurant at Benson University. He called it the Undergrad Grill. Tom had wanted to open a restaurant at Benson for several months but was waiting for the right location to become available. He was very pleased when he was able to rent suitable space on Restaurant Row. He figured that this would be a great location and well worth the high rent and all the renovations he needed to do on the building. Since he wanted to open the restaurant as soon as possible, he hired the first people he could find to do the renovations and painting. He ended up paying the workers more than the going rate in order to get the job done as quickly as possible. When the time came to open, he didn't have enough money to do much advertising. However, since his restaurant was surrounded by many other restaurants and since there were over 25,000 undergraduate and graduate students looking for a place to eat, Higgins was certain his restaurant would do well even without advertising. After placing several help-wanted ads in the local newspaper, Higgins hired two waitresses to work for him. He couldn't afford professional cooks, so he hired several students to do the cooking.

Unfortunately for Higgins, the competition was more intense than he had anticipated. After two months, his restaurant was not doing very well. One of his waitresses had quit and the number of customers was decreasing.

A. Discuss this case in small groups. What problems do you see with the way Higgins is managing his restaurant?

Problems

1. _____
2. _____
3. _____
4. _____
5. _____
6. _____

B. What steps can Higgins take to solve his problems and increase business?

Solutions

1. _____
2. _____
3. _____
4. _____
5. _____
6. _____

C. Write a one-paragraph report describing your proposed solutions and suggestions. Begin by briefly stating the problem.

D. Exchange paragraphs with a classmate to revise and edit.

Analyzing a Problem/Solution Essay

Read the essay below and answer the questions that follow.

Energy Sources: A Dilemma for the Twenty-First Century

All of us have come to expect that reliable sources of energy will be available forever. We drive our cars wherever and whenever we want. When the gas tank gets low, we simply pull into the nearest gas station. At home, whenever we need to change the temperature, prepare food, listen to music, or watch TV, we simply turn on the nearest appliance. What is the source of all this energy that we use so carelessly? In most of the world, energy is created by burning fossil fuels—coal, natural gas, and oil. The problem is that these resources are finite. At our current rate of use, we will be out of petroleum in 30 to 40 years. That means that if you are under the age of 40, the day will probably come when you will not have gasoline for your car or electricity for your appliances. The three most commonly proposed solutions to this worldwide problem are increasing the efficiency of appliances and vehicles, improving conservation efforts, and finding alternative energy sources.

The first solution, improving the efficiency of appliances and vehicles, is something that manufacturers have been working on for two decades. For instance, televisions now use 65 to 75 percent less electricity than they did in the 1970s, refrigerators use 20 to 30 percent less electricity, and cars need less gas to travel more miles. Unfortunately, there are so many more televisions, refrigerators, and cars in the world now that overall consumption continues to rise.

Another solution to the dangerous energy situation is to improve our conservation efforts. For example, all of us must get in the habit of recycling whatever we can. We have to install high-efficiency lightbulbs in our homes and offices and turn off the lights in rooms that we are not using. It would also help if we biked, walked, carpooled, or used public transportation more and used our cars less. Unfortunately, improvements in both conservation and efficiency are only temporary solutions. They extend the useful life of our current fuels, but they do not explain what we will do when these fuels run out.

The best solution, then, is to find alternative sources of energy to meet our future needs. The current leading alternatives to fossil fuels are fusion and solar energy. Fusion is a nuclear reaction that results in an enormous release of energy. It is practically pollution-free and is probably our best long-range option. Unfortunately, it will not be available for at least 20 years. The other possible energy source, solar power, is really the source of all energy, except nuclear, on Earth. When people think of solar energy, they generally think of the many ways that individual homeowners can utilize the power of the sun for heating water and buildings. But solar energy can also be utilized to generate electricity and to purify fuels for automobiles.

It is clear that for us to have sufficient energy resources for the twenty-first century, it will be necessary to pursue the development and encourage the use of alternative energy sources worldwide. If we ignore this problem, what will become of our children? What will life be like for them in the year 2050?

Pair Work

Answer the following questions with a partner:

1. What is the thesis statement of the essay?
2. What three solutions to the energy shortage does the author propose?
3. What examples does the author use to describe each solution?
4. How are the body paragraphs arranged?
5. What technique(s) did the author use in writing the conclusion?

Essay Plan: Problem/Solution

The guidelines below will help you remember what you need to do in each part of a problem/solution essay.

Introduction

1. Provide background information about the problem.
2. Describe the problem and state why it is serious.
3. Identify possible solutions.

Supporting Paragraphs

1. Discuss one solution in each supporting paragraph.
2. Explain the positive and negative aspects of each solution.
3. Provide details to explain each solution.
4. Organize the paragraphs according to order of importance.

Conclusion

1. Summarize the solutions.
2. Draw a conclusion or make a prediction based on your suggestions.

Writing a Problem/Solution Essay

In this activity, you will practice writing an essay that analyzes the solutions to a problem. Follow these steps:

a. Prewriting
Choose one of the following topics and freewrite about it for 10 minutes. Use a separate piece of paper if you do not have enough room here.

1. Sexism
2. The generation gap
3. War
4. Smog
5. Racism

(continued on next page)

b. Planning

Use your freewriting as a basis for planning your essay. Identify several of your solutions that you think you can develop into an essay. If you have not generated enough ideas, do another, more focused freewriting. Then prepare an informal outline of your essay.

c. Drafting

On a separate piece of paper, write the first draft of your essay. Refer to the essay plan on page 113 to help you with your draft. Be sure to provide some background information on the problem in the introduction and include a clear thesis statement. Organize the body paragraphs according to order of importance, beginning or ending with the most important solution. End with a conclusion that summarizes the solutions, draws a conclusion, or makes a prediction.

d. Personal Revising

Use the checklist on page 54 to revise the first draft. Be sure that all your paragraphs are unified and coherent. Also, check to make sure you have provided enough support to explain each solution fully. Write or type a revised version of your essay.

e. Peer Revising

Exchange papers with a classmate. Read your partner's essay and use the following questions to help you with the revision process:

1. What are some interesting things you learned from reading this essay?
2. Did the introduction provide enough background information to explain the problem?
3. How many solutions did the author offer in the essay? Is each solution adequately developed in a separate body paragraph?
4. Are the paragraphs arranged in a logical order? What type of order did the author use?
5. Did the author use transitions to guide you from one idea to the next? Were there any irrelevant sentences that should be eliminated?
6. Did the author include a conclusion that summarizes the solutions or makes a prediction?

Incorporate any suggestions your classmate has made that you agree with.

f. Editing

Use the checklist on page 65 to edit your essay. Correct all the grammar, punctuation, capitalization, and spelling errors before you copy it over or type it.

You Be the Editor

The following paragraph contains seven mistakes. Find the mistakes and correct them. Then copy the corrected paragraph onto a separate sheet of paper.

If you are like most people, you average one to three colds per year. Even if you do not have a cold right now. The chances are three in four that within the next year, at least one cold virus will find you. then you'll spend a week or so suffering from the miseries of the common cold: fatigue, sore throat, laryngitis, sneezing, stuffy or runny nose, and coughing. According to researchers, colds are the most common medical reason for missing school and work. Once you catch a cold, what can you do. There is no known cure yet for a cold. There are, however, several thing you can do to suppress the symptom's so that you feel better while the virus runs its course. For example, make sure that you get plenty of sleep and drink lots of liquids. You may find commercially available cold remedies such as decongestants, cough suppressants, and expectorants helpful, but keep in mind that these products can cause side effects. Many people prefer home remedies such as chicken soup, garlic, and ginger tea. In treating a cold, remember the wisdom of the ages, "if you treat a cold, it will be gone in a week; if you don't treat it, will be gone in seven days."

Source: *Jane Brody's Cold and Flu Fighter*

On Your Own

Write a problem/solution essay based on one of the problems you analyzed in the Examining Solutions section on pages 106 and 107. Be sure your essay has an introduction that describes the problem, several body paragraphs that explain the solutions, and a conclusion that summarizes the solutions or makes a prediction.

Writing Summaries

Preparing a summary requires a special kind of writing. Unlike the other types of writing you have done in this book, a summary should not include any of your own personal ideas. The only purpose of a summary is to condense what another author has written. This means reducing what the author has said to its main points.

Summaries are used in academic writing for every field. For example, in a business class, you might be asked to summarize an article from the *Wall Street Journal.* In a chemistry or physics class, a summary format is often used to prepare lab reports. In a literature class, you might be required to write summaries of novels or short stories.

Summarizing an Article

A good summary should present a clear, concise idea of the main points of an article to someone who has not read it. In order to write an effective summary, you need to have a true understanding of the original article. This means taking the time to read the article carefully to determine the author's purpose, thesis, and main supporting points.

How to Write a One-Paragraph Summary

1. Read the article once to determine the author's thesis.
2. Reread the article and take notes on the main points.
3. Using your notes as a guide, write the first draft of your summary. It should include:

   a. A topic sentence that states the name of the article, the author, and the source. It should also include the main point of the article.
   b. A body that focuses on explaining, in your own words, the main ideas presented in the article. An effective way to do this is by answering the questions *what, where, when, who,* and *why.*
   c. A final statement that summarizes any conclusions the author made in the article.

4. Revise the draft of your summary. Check to see that you have accurately summarized the author's main ideas. If you included any of the author's minor points, eliminate them. In addition, be sure that you did not include any of your own thoughts or opinions about the topic.
5. Edit your summary to make sure that the grammar, spelling, punctuation, and capitalization are correct.

Analyzing a One-Paragraph Summary

Read the article "The Growing of Green Cars" and complete the exercise that follows.

THE GROWING OF GREEN CARS

Every year, more than a million new cars and trucks hit U.S. highways. They join the countless vehicles already on the road. And each one adds to the pollution that darkens our skies.

But that soon may change: On the horizon are cars that make little or no pollution at all. They are called "green cars," because they are friendly to our green earth.

Most car engines burn gasoline, which adds to the "smog" that dirties our cities. This air pollution—nitrogen oxide, carbon monoxide and more—hurts humans. It also rises high in the sky where it soaks up heat from the sun. Some scientists say this causes a second problem: the "greenhouse effect," or warming of the earth. The air has become so bad in California that the state passed a new pollution law. It tells auto makers that some of their new cars must not pollute at all. They will be zero-emission vehicles, or ZEV. Five years from now, in 1998, two of every 100 new cars sold in California must be ZEV. The requirement shoots to one in 10 just after the turn of the century.

California does not suffer smog alone. According to the U.S. Environmental Protection Agency (EPA), vehicles nationwide cause 56 percent of cancer-causing air pollutants. "While today's cars *are* 80 percent cleaner than 20 years ago," says the EPA's Martha Casey, "we have more cars today."

Today, the average family minivan gets only 23 miles per gallon. Some lawmakers in the U.S. Congress want cars nationwide to do better—averaging 40 miles per gallon. That would produce less smog per mile traveled.

But reaching that goal will be costly. The Honda Civic VX, for example, gets an astounding 48 miles per gallon. But the equipment making that possible adds almost $2,500 to the car's price. Few customers want to pay the extra cost. Honda sells far more of a cheaper Civic model that burns more gasoline.

Burning less fuel is one way to cut pollution. Another way is to tune engines so they can burn cleaner fuels. These cars, called Flexible Fuel Vehicles, may run on gasoline, hydrogen, methanol, ethanol, natural gas, propane gas, or various other fuels. Still, these fuels must be burned. And burning causes pollution.

Electric cars don't burn fuel, so they put out no exhaust at all. They are the cars that companies will build to comply with the stiff, new ZEV laws.

Already, companies from Chrysler to Mercedes-Benz put electric motors in some of their current models, with all new designs to follow.

But some people argue that even electric cars aren't perfect. Why? Because the batteries that run them get their energy from power plants. And power plants often belch their own pollutants into the air.

Both lawmakers and auto makers agree that there are no easy answers on the road to perhaps the perfect ZEV: an electric car powered by the sun. Much more work is needed to make such an earth-friendly car practical.

But with each step—such as models free of chlorofluorocarbon—cars get better.

They will have to. Almost a dozen Northeastern states and Washington, D.C., are adopting California's tough auto standards. That, by one manufacturer's estimate, means nearly 300,000 electric cars in the United States by 2001—proof that green cars are taking root. ♦

Boys' Life, May 1993

Here are four summaries of the article. Read the summaries and decide which one is the best.

Summary 1

"The Growing of Green Cars" describes the serious pollution problem in California and many other states. Since cars and trucks add to the pollution, auto makers are trying to design cars that are environmentally safer.

(continued on next page)

Summary 2

This article is about how car companies are finally trying to deal with the pollution that their products cause. Since cars and trucks around the country are responsible for over 50 percent of the dangerous pollutants in the air we breathe, it is about time that the automobile companies decided to do something to make their vehicles safer for the environment. California has recently passed a law that requires auto makers to produce a certain amount of cars that do not pollute the environment at all. Other states are following in California's footsteps and hopefully, by the year 2000, many cars on the road will not burn any fuel at all. These new electric cars may be the answer to the serious problem of pollution caused by burning fuel.

Summary 3

In "The Growing of Green Cars" (*Boys' Life,* May 1993), W. E. Butterworth discusses the new trends in environmentally safe automobiles called "green cars." Auto makers are working hard to produce cars that cause less pollution. Their long-term goal is to make zero-emission vehicles (ZEV) to comply with new state laws. The author mentions several ways that car companies can reach their goal, such as designing cars that burn less fuel, tuning engines so they burn cleaner fuels, and producing electric cars that do not burn any fuel. However, none of these solutions is perfect, and all of them are expensive. Although everyone agrees that there are no simple solutions, more and more states are adopting stricter antipollution laws.

Summary 4

In "The growing of Green Cars" (*Boys' Life,* May 1993), W. E. Butterworth describes the ways that cars and trucks add to the already high level of air pollution in the United States. According to the U.S. Environmental Protection Agency (EPA), vehicles nationwide cause 56 percent of cancer-causing air pollutants. This may soon change as states like California pass laws that require auto makers to produce cars that cause less pollution. The long-term goal is to make zero-emission vehicles (ZEV) that will not pollute the air at all. Within five years, 2 percent of all cars sold in California must be ZEV. This will increase to 10 percent by the year 2000. Even though cars today are 80 percent cleaner than those produced 20 years ago, the problem is worse because of the great increase in the number of cars on the road. The article mentions several ways to cut pollution caused by cars. One way is to produce cars that burn less fuel. A second way is to tune engines so they burn cleaner fuels, such as hydrogen, methanol, ethanol, natural gas, or propane gas. Finally, automobile companies are designing electric cars that do not burn any fuel. Companies such as Chrysler and Mercedes-Benz are already putting electric motors into some of their cars.

1. Which of the four summaries is the best? Why?

     _____

     _____

2. Analyze the other three summaries and determine what kinds of mistakes the authors made.

     Summary _____

     _____

     _____

Summary _____

_____

_____

Summary _____

_____

_____

Completing a One-Paragraph Summary

Read the article "New Planet May Support Life" and complete the summary that follows.

Ready to Write

NEW PLANET MAY SUPPORT LIFE

by David L. Chandler

San Antonio—Astronomers announced to stunned colleagues yesterday the first discovery of a planet outside the solar system that may be capable of supporting life.

The find brings humankind to "a gateway to a new era in science," said Geoffrey W. Marcy, an astronomer at San Francisco State University and one of the two scientists who reported finding the planet. We now know, he said, that the Earth "has cousins in other solar systems. . . . Planets aren't rare, after all."

The discovery of the planet, in the constellation Virgo, culminates centuries of speculation and years of searching that produced a few intriguing results but never any sign of a planet resembling those in the solar system.

The planet, more than six times the size of Jupiter, orbits a star called 70 Virginis, which is almost a twin of the sun. And the planet's distance from that star—less than half the Earth's distance from the sun—suggests that it is likely to have a surface temperature of about 185 degrees Fahrenheit. That means that liquid water, the basis of all life as we know it, could exist there.

The find was one of two, and possibly three, planets outside the solar system whose discoveries were reported here yesterday at a meeting of the American Astronomical Society. The first confirmed sighting of a planet outside the solar system was announced by a Swiss team only three months ago.

"The exciting thing is that we found a planet where water could exist," said NASA administrator Daniel Goldin, who has made searching for other planets and indications of possible life elsewhere a top priority for the space agency. "On Earth, wherever we find water, we find life."

Robert Brown, an astronomer at the Space Telescope Science Institute and a specialist in planet formation, said, "What we are seeing here is the culmination of 500 years of intellectual history" that began when Copernicus found that the Earth was not the center of the universe. ♦

Boston Globe, Jan. 18, 1996

In "New Planet May Support Life" (*Boston Globe,* January 18, 1996),

_____ reports the first discovery made by

astronomers of _____ that might be able to

support life. This planet _____

_____

_____. Because the planet probably has a surface

temperature of _____,

experts believe it could _____.

Scientists are very excited about this discovery because _____

_____.

Writing a One-Paragraph Summary

Complete the following steps to write a one-paragraph summary of "Violent Crime on the Rise."

a. Reading
Read the article "Violent Crime on the Rise" once to determine the author's thesis.

Thesis

_____

_____

VIOLENT CRIME ON THE RISE
by Thomas Campbell

Homicides cause the deaths of more children in Washington, D.C. than any other single type of injury, including car accidents, house fires, or drowning. Unfortunately, this is not an exclusive phenomenon of Washington. The overcrowded neighborhoods of many big American cities, such as New York, Detroit, Miami, Chicago, and Los Angeles, are all plagued with senseless violent crime. Types of violent crime range from arson and burglary to assault, rape, and murder. The solution to this growing problem is not to build more and bigger prisons, but rather to examine and deal with the causes: easy access to guns, constant craving for drugs, and overwhelming poverty.

An obvious trigger to violence is easy access to guns and firearms. Handguns are by far the most common murder weapon, accounting for 13,352 murders in the United States last year. Since almost anyone in the U.S. can buy a gun, the number of violent crimes involving guns is very high and continues to grow. For example, murders involving guns in New York City are more than thirty times what they were a half a century ago. In 1995 alone, there were 1,946 murders involving guns in New York City.

Drugs are also responsible for much of the violent crime that plagues American cities. Most inner-city crimes are drug related in some way. Many violent crimes involve drug buyers and sellers who are fighting. Others are committed by people acting under the influence of drugs, or thieves looking for money to buy drugs. Still other violent crimes are the result of territorial disputes between drug dealers.

In addition to the prevalence of guns and drugs in the large urban areas of the U.S., the overwhelming poverty that afflicts many residents has a direct link to the amount of crime. No matter what the causes of poverty, the effect is always the same: people lack basic necessities such as adequate nutrition, housing, education, and medical care. As feelings of helplessness and frustration turn into anger, violent crime can become an increasingly serious problem for society.

People commit violent crimes for many different reasons. The question is, how can we as a society deal with this problem? Many experts feel that punishment is the best way to deter crime. Others feel that the best way to reduce crime is to rehabilitate criminals. Because criminals vary greatly in the kind of crimes they commit, their emotional stability, and their socioeconomic backgrounds, there probably is no one best way to solve the problem of violent crime. It is obvious, however, that education, stricter gun laws, and tighter controls on drugs would help reduce violent crime. ◆

Detroit Today ◆ *January 30*

b. Planning
Read the article again and take notes on the important points.

c. Drafting
On a separate piece of paper, write a first draft of your summary. Include only the main points of the article. Try to answer the questions *what, where, when, who,* and *why.*

d. Personal Revising
On a separate piece of paper, write a revised draft of your summary.

(continued on next page)

e. Peer Revising

Exchange papers with a classmate. Read your partner's summary and help him or her revise it. Use the following checklist as a guide:

1. Does the summary begin with a sentence that states the name, author, and source of the article and that identifies the thesis?
2. Does the summary present the author's main ideas?
3. Was the writer careful not to include any minor details or personal opinions?
4. Does the summary end with a statement that summarizes the author's conclusion?

f. Editing

Edit your revised draft for correct grammar, punctuation, spelling, and capitalization. Copy your summary onto another piece of paper.

More Practice Writing One-Paragraph Summaries

1. Read the following article about Franklin Delano Roosevelt (FDR) and the disease that handicapped him eleven years before he was elected president of the United States in 1932. Despite his disability, FDR was the only American president to be elected four times. He led the United States during the Great Depression and through World War II.

POLITICS AS USUAL
by Diana Childress

When polio paralyzed Franklin Roosevelt in August 1921, he put on a brave front. Having learned from childhood to bear pain "without fuss," he joked about a thirty-nine-year-old man getting a baby's disease and radiated optimism about his recovery. "The doctors say," he wrote a friend in December, "that by this Spring I will be walking without any limp."

But as Franklin's wife, Eleanor, said later, "I know that he had real fear when he was first taken ill." Polio was "a trial by fire." A big question in everyone's mind was how this crippling blow would affect Franklin's future in politics.

For Sara Roosevelt, the answer was perfectly clear. Her son, she felt, had already served his country well. With her money to support him, he could retire to the family home in Hyde Park and enjoy his business interests and hobbies.

Sara's views were typical of the times. In the early 1900s, people with physical disabilities were treated like invalids, either hospitalized or kept at home. Many thought it "bad manners" for a disabled person to appear in public. The idea of a "cripple" pursuing a political career was unthinkable.

Eleanor also doubted that her husband could ever return to public office. But she knew how important Franklin's political ambitions were to him. The doctors told her that keeping hope alive would improve his chances of recovery. Taking an active part in life, even if it tired him, was "better for his condition," they said. So she encouraged and helped him to stay involved in politics.

Louis Howe, Franklin's long-time political adviser, added his support. Within days after falling ill, Franklin was dictating letters that he could not even sign because the paralysis had temporarily spread to his arms and thumbs. He agreed to become a member of the executive committee of the Democratic party in New York State even though at that time, as one biographer notes, he was lying in bed and "working for hours to try to wiggle a big toe."

With Howe's help, Franklin kept the general public from finding out how seriously ill he was. Meanwhile, he worked feverishly to try to regain the use of his legs. Determined to make a full recovery, he spent much of his time exercising and struggling to learn to walk.

Cobblestone, April 1995

When Democratic leaders urged him to run for U.S. senator or governor of New York in 1922, he had to admit he was not ready. Yet he kept busy on the sidelines, writing letters and articles while Howe and Eleanor appeared for him in public.

In 1924, Franklin could not avoid the Democratic National Convention and still be taken seriously as a politician. The agile man who had vaulted over a row of chairs to reach the speaker's platform in 1920 now inched painfully forward on crutches. "But nothing was the matter with his voice or his enthusiasm," wrote a reporter. His half-hour speech nominating Al Smith for president was cheered for one hour thirteen minutes.

Four years later, Franklin still hoped that another year or two of rehabilitation would free him from his wheelchair and crutches. He tried to avoid the calls from the New York State Democratic Convention urging him to accept the nomination for governor. But when the Democratic presidential candidate, Al Smith, finally got him on the line, he realized he could no longer plead illness without letting his party down.

Franklin Roosevelt's return to active politics in spite of his inability to walk was a major triumph for himself and for disabled people everywhere. He never achieved full recovery, but his years of hard work brought a maturity and a depth of understanding that enhanced his greatness as a leader. ♦

(continued on next page)

Reread the article and take notes on the important points. Write a one-paragraph summary based on your notes. Remember to revise and edit your summary before you hand it in.

2. Read the following newspaper article about the retirement of basketball hero Larry Bird, the star forward of the Boston Celtics. Then summarize the article in one paragraph.

LARRY BIRD: A BASKETBALL LEGEND

*L*arry Bird, considered by many experts the greatest all-around basketball player in history, made it official yesterday. He is retiring from the Boston Celtics because of injuries to his back. The basketball world is in mourning. Why are so many people mourning the retirement of someone who used to shoot basketballs for a living? There are many reasons. First of all, Larry Joe Bird did much more than shoot basketballs. He was an inspiration to everyone who played with or against him. He once said, "I can't run and I can't jump, but I sure can play basketball." His friend and former rival, Magic Johnson, has said that Larry can dominate a game without even taking a shot, by doing all the other little things that help a team win. He was the kind of player who made everyone around him play better because he was so unselfish with the ball. He gave electrifying performances on the court and was one of the best play makers that the game has ever known.

Bird had awesome talent when it came to shooting, rebounding, and passing the ball. Although we admire all these talents, they are not the reason that Larry Bird is the idol of so many. The real reason is that he was a total team player. He involved everyone in the game. He set the tempo for everyone and his confidence was contagious. The other reason has to do with his exemplary work habits. Respected for his drive and focus, Bird has been called one of the world's most dedicated athletes. Larry loved the game of basketball and practiced tirelessly, regularly taking 300 practice shots before a game. He also loved a challenge. His teammate M. L. Carr once said, "Larry sets goals that are unreachable for the rest of us. Then he surpasses them." He was a fierce competitor, but his single-minded tenacity and pride in being the best he could be meant that he never gave up.

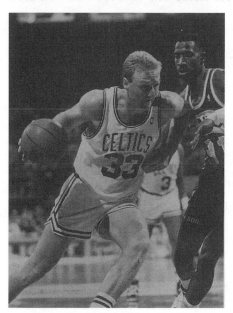

Larry retires having amassed an impressive record of statistics. He carried his college team, the little-known Indiana State Sycamores to a championship season in 1978. The following year he joined the Boston Celtics and won the Rookie of the Year Award, leading the Celtics to 61 victories, 32 more than they had won the previous season. This feat ranks as one of the best turnaround stories in National Basketball Association (NBA) history. He led the Celtics to three world championships. Bird is one of only three people to receive the Most Valuable Player (MVP) Award for three straight seasons: 1984, 1985, and 1986. Larry won the Playoff MVP Award twice, in 1984 and 1986. He was a twelve-time All Star and four-time winner of the All Star Three-Point Shooting Contest. He was the first player in history to shoot over 50 percent from field-goal range and 90 percent from the foul line. Larry has over 5,000 assists to his credit. As co-captain of the original "Dream Team," he led the U.S. to victory, winning a gold medal at the 1992 Olympic Games in Barcelona, Spain.

As Larry Bird retires from basketball, the sport loses one of its brightest stars—not only for the pure skills he brought to the game, but more importantly for the inspiration that he brought to both players and fans. Because of his skills, his work ethic, his value system, and his deep understanding of team dynamics, he will always be known as "Larry Legend." ♦

You Be the Editor

The following letter contains six mistakes. Find the mistakes and correct them. Then copy the letter onto a separate piece of paper.

Judy Johnson
123 Rolling Way
Peekskill, Oregon 00000

Dear Helene,

I just finished reading one of the best books I have ever read. It is called One Hundred Years of Solitude and was written by Gabriel García Márquez. He won the Nobel Prize for this book in 1982. It was first published in 1967 in Argentina and translated into english in 1970. Briefly, it is the story of the fictional town of Macondo as seen through the eyes of many generations of the Buendía family. We learn about the changes that the town goes through as it grow and the years roll by we also read about the universal themes of birth, death, love, war, wealth, poverty, honor and corruption as we spend time with this large and fascinating family. The writing is simple, yet beautiful, even in translation. If you are looking for a really good book to read, recommend this book to you. Let me know if you read it. I hope that you enjoy reading about these people and their lives as much as I did.

Love,

Judy

On Your Own

Choose a newspaper or magazine article on any topic that interests you. Read it carefully and write a one-paragraph summary of it. Bring the article and your summary to class to share with your classmates.

Personal Expression

You will often be asked to write about your reaction to something you have read, seen, or heard. When you write a reaction, begin by briefly summarizing the original material. Then give your opinion about it. For example, if you are asked to react to an article, begin by summarizing it in a few sentences before stating your personal opinion.

Reaction papers have a very important place in academic writing. In many classes you will be required to react to something you have read, heard, or seen. For example, in a literature class, a professor might ask for your reaction to a poem or short story. In a music class, an assignment could involve writing a reaction to a piece of music. Professors frequently ask for your reactions on essay tests.

Writing Reactions

1. Read the following newspaper article about two convicted murderers who were put to death for crimes they had been convicted of committing many years before.

What Is Justice?

TWO MEN WERE PUT TO DEATH last week in the United States for murders that they had been convicted of committing many years ago. Billy Bailey died in the first hanging in Delaware in fifty years. It was twenty years ago that he murdered an elderly couple after breaking into their home. John Taylor, a child rapist and murderer, was shot by a five-man firing squad in Utah.

Polls show that 70 to 80 percent of U.S. citizens favor capital punishment. Many believe that people who commit horrendous crimes deserve to die brutally in return for the brutality that they inflicted on their victims. Others protest the barbarism of the death penalty, be it by lethal injection, electric chair, firing squad, or hanging. While there were many people who supported the two deaths that took place last week, there were also many protesters.

In small groups discuss the article and answer the following questions:

    a. What is your opinion about capital punishment? Do you think there are any situations where it is an appropriate method of punishment?

    b. Do you think capital punishment deters crime? Why or why not?

    c. Do you know of another country that uses capital punishment? Why does or why doesn't that country use it?

On a separate piece of paper, write a letter to the editor of a newspaper expressing your opinion about the use of capital punishment in cases such as the two described in the article.

Share your letter with the members of your group.

2. Write a reaction to one of the articles in Chapter 10. Begin your reaction with a one- or two-sentence summary of the article.

3. Read the following memo and complete the exercise that follows.

You are married to one of the managers of a small computer company in San Francisco, California. Your spouse has just received the memo that follows.

MEMO

TO: All Employees

FROM: Jim Philips

RE: Merger with Logicom

DATE: June 30

As most of you know, we have been talking for several months now with the people at Logicom about merging our two companies. We are pleased to announce that the details have been worked out and we will be combining our companies. The official merger date is set for October 5. We are confident that we can look forward to a long and successful alliance with Logicom, since our products are so complementary to one another. This merger should lead to greater success in the marketplace than either company could achieve on its own.

This memo is also to confirm that as per Logicom's insistence, we will be moving our offices and people to Burlington, Massachusetts. We know that this will be difficult and disruptive for some of you, but we sincerely believe that it is in the best interests of the company. We hope that each and every one of you will join us in this exciting opportunity. Further details regarding the merger and the move will be sent to you shortly.

Write a letter to your parents or a close friend summarizing the memo and expressing your reaction to this news.

Dear _____ ,

Love,

_____

Reacting to Visual Stimuli

In the previous exercises, you have been reacting to written material. On the following pages, you will have the opportunity to practice reacting to visual material.

1. Look at the two photos.

(continued on next page)

2. Answer the following questions:

    a. Describe what is happening in each photo.

    b. Which photo do you like better? Why?

    c. Which photo has more meaning for you? Why?

    d. Which photo would you find it easier to write about?

3. On a separate piece of paper, write a reaction to one of the photos. Begin by describing what you see in the photo. Then discuss how the image makes you feel and what you think it means. Bring your own life experiences to your written reaction.

4. Exchange papers with someone who chose the same photo you did. Compare and contrast your reactions. Then help each other revise and edit before you give your papers to your teacher.

Art

John Singleton Copley was one of the most important North American painters of the eighteenth century. Copley is best known as a master portrait painter. During the second half of his career, he painted huge and dramatic paintings based on important events of his time. His expert skills as a portraitist made his paintings very realistic.

"Watson and the Shark" is one of Copley's most memorable works. It tells the true story of a man named Watson who was attacked by a shark while he was swimming in Havana Harbor. Watson was dramatically rescued and later asked Copley

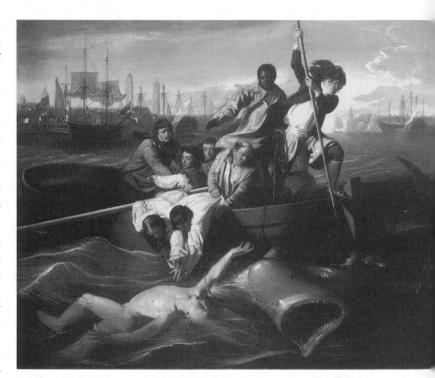

to translate the gruesome story into a painting. Copley made it as realistic as he could. Some art historians think that the shark symbolizes evil and that the man rescuing Watson symbolizes good. They believe that Watson himself symbolizes the way we all struggle between the forces of good and evil. Discuss the painting with your classmates and answer the questions that follow:

    a. What do you see when you look at the painting? Describe the people and their surroundings. You may need to use your dictionary.

    b. What is happening in the painting?

    c. What feelings does the painting evoke in you?

Writing a Response to the Painting

1. Choose one of the following topics to write about. Begin with a short description of the painting.

    a. Write a story based on ideas you got from the painting.

    b. Write about your emotional reaction when you look at the painting.

    c. Discuss the ways the painting symbolizes the conflict between good and evil.

2. Exchange your reaction with a classmate to revise and edit.
3. Copy your revised draft onto a separate piece of paper to hand in to your teacher.

Andrew Wyeth is another important North American painter. He is known for his realistic interpretations of people and landscapes, his technical brilliance, and his affection for his subjects. He found inspiration in his everyday surroundings.

One of Wyeth's best-known paintings is called "Christina's World." Discuss your impressions of the painting with your classmates and answer the questions that follow:

   a. What do you see when you look at the painting? Describe the woman and her surroundings. You may need to use your dictionary.
   b. What seems to be happening in the painting?
   c. What story do you think the artist is trying to tell?
   d. What adjectives would you use to describe the painting?

Writing a Response to the Painting

1. Choose one of the following topics to write about. Begin with a short description of what you see.

   a. What story do you think the artist is telling in this painting?
   b. Write your own story based on ideas you got from the painting.
   c. What do you think about when you look at the painting?
   d. What is your opinion of the painting? Explain.

2. Exchange your reaction with a classmate to revise and edit.
3. Copy your revised and edited draft onto a separate sheet of paper to hand in to your teacher.

FOLLOW-UP ACTIVITY

"Christina's World" depicts one of Wyeth's neighbors, a woman named Christina who was paralyzed. Wyeth's belief that life contains hardship and suffering is reflected by Christina, who stretches awkwardly toward the farmhouse that is beyond her ability to reach. Art experts point out the mood of despair and the sense of frustration in the painting. They think this painting is about life's limitations and unattainable goals.

Look at the painting again, now that you know the story behind it. Answer the following questions:

1. What aspects of the painting express a mood of despair and a sense of frustration?

_____

_____

(continued on next page)

2. Do you see that the painting is about life's limitations and unattainable goals? Why or why not?

_____

_____

_____

3. What is your reaction to the painting now that you know the story that Wyeth was trying to tell? Write a paragraph explaining your reaction.

_____

_____

_____

_____

_____

_____

_____

_____

_____

Reacting to Quotations

Many writing assignments involve responding to quotations. You will often be asked to explain the meaning of a quotation and then give your opinion of it.

A. Read the following quotations from around the world and put a checkmark next to those that you find especially interesting. In small groups, discuss the quotes that all the members of your group checked.

_____ 1. Patience is power. (Chinese proverb)

_____ 2. It is very tiring to hate. (Jean Rostand)

_____ 3. We are shaped by what we love. (Goethe)

_____ 4. Jealousy is a tiger that tears not only its prey but also its own raging heart. (Michael Beer)

_____ 5. Happiness sneaks in through a door you didn't know you left open. (John Barrymore)

_____ 6. Humility is the root, mother, nurse, foundation, and bond of all virtue. (John Chrysostom)

_____ 7. Winning is neither everything nor the only thing; it is one of many things. (Joan Benoit Samuelson)

_____ 8. Imitation is the sincerest form of flattery. (Nathaniel Cotton)

_____ 9. A human life is like a letter of the alphabet. It can be meaningless. Or it can be part of a great meaning. (Anonymous)

_____ 10. The poorest way to face life is to face it with a sneer. (Theodore Roosevelt)

_____ 11. A wise man will make more opportunities than he finds. (Francis Bacon)

_____ 12. There is no such thing as civilized warfare. (William Allen White)

_____ 13. Nothing is really work unless you would rather be doing something else. (Sir James Matthew Barrie)

_____ 14. I hate television. I hate it as much as I hate peanuts. But I can't stop eating peanuts. (Orson Welles)

_____ 15. Victory belongs to the most persevering. (Napoleon Bonaparte)

_____ 16. Money and time are the heaviest burdens of life, and the unhappiest of all mortals are those who have more of either than they can use. (Samuel Johnson)

B. Choose one of the quotes you discussed with your group and write a one-paragraph reaction to it. Be sure to include the quote at the beginning of your paragraph and thoroughly explain why you chose that quote and how it has meaning for you.

C. Read your reactions to the other members of your group for their feedback. Then revise, edit, and copy your reaction over before handing it in.

Writing a Reaction to Poetry

1. Robert Frost (1874–1963) is one of the most important North American poets of the twentieth century. Frost was awarded the Pulitzer Prize for poetry four times and in 1961, at the inauguration of John F. Kennedy, he became the first poet to read one of his own poems at a presidential inauguration. Frost's poetry, with its emphasis on nature, is still immensely popular today.

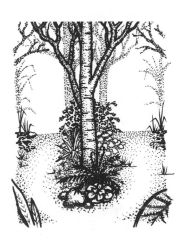

"The Road Not Taken" tells the story of an important choice the author made in his life. Read the poem and do the activities that follow.

The Road Not Taken

I. Two roads diverged in a yellow wood,[1]
And sorry I could not travel both
And be one traveler, long I stood
And looked down one as far as I could
To where it bent in the undergrowth;[2]

II. Then took the other, as just as fair,[3]
And having perhaps the better claim,
Because it was grassy and wanted wear;[4]
Though as for that the passing there
Had worn them really about the same,

III. And both that morning equally lay
In leaves no step had trodden black.[5]
Oh I kept the first for another day!
Yet knowing how way leads on to way,[6]
I doubted if I should ever come back.

IV. I shall be telling this with a sigh
Somewhere ages and ages hence:[7]
Two roads diverged in a wood, and I—
I took the one less traveled by,
And that has made all the
    difference.

—Robert Frost

[1] One road divided into two roads in a forest
[2] To the place where it turned under the low bushes
[3] I took the other road which was just as nice
[4] Because it was slightly overgrown and less used
[5] No one had walked on either road yet that day
[6] I knew how one road often leads to another road
[7] In some place in the future

Understanding the Poem

The four stanzas (groups of lines) of the poem each tell a part of the story. Read each stanza again and think about what it means. Then look at the following summaries. Each summary refers to one of the stanzas in the poem. Match each summary with the stanza it refers to.

a. He decided to take the road that looked like it had not been used as much.

Stanza ——————————

b. Sometime in the future, he will remember this day when he had to make a choice and be glad that he took the road that was less traveled.

Stanza ——————————

c. A man was walking in the woods and he came to a place where the single road divided into two separate roads. He was sorry that he could not take both roads.

Stanza ——————————

d. Although he chose the second road, he hoped that he would be able to return some day to take the first one. But he doubted that he ever would.

Stanza ——————————

Responding to the Poem

Robert Frost's poem is based on a choice he had to make. Think about an important choice that you have made. On a separate piece of paper, describe the situation and the effect your choice has had on your life.

2. Emily Dickinson (1830–1886) is another of North America's gifted poets. Although she wrote over 1,775 poems, only seven of them were published during her lifetime. In her unique style of poetry, Dickinson explored aspects of love, life, death, nature, and immortality.

"Hope Is the Thing with Feathers" is one of Dickinson's most famous poems. In this poem, she uses the metaphor of a bird to describe her feelings about hope. Read the poem and do the exercises that follow.

Hope Is the Thing with Feathers

Hope is the thing with feathers
That perches[1] in the soul,
And sings the tune without the words,
And never stops at all.

And sweetest in the gale[2] is heard;
And sore must be the storm
That could abash[3] the little bird
That kept so many warm.

I've heard it in the chillest land,
And on the strangest sea;
Yet, never, in extremity[4],
It asked a crumb[5] of me.

—Emily Dickinson

[1] sits
[2] strong wind
[3] upset
[4] an extreme situation
[5] a small piece of food

Writing Metaphors

A metaphor is a phrase that describes something by comparing it to something else without the words *like* or *as*. Reread the first two lines of Emily Dickinson's poem. Using these lines as a model, create your own metaphors for each of the following words.

EXAMPLE:

　　Happiness is a flower with buds that blossoms in my heart.

1. Jealousy is a/an _____ with _____

   that _____

2. Beauty is a/an _____ with _____

   that _____

3. Hate is a/an _____ with _____ that

   _____

4. Love is a/an _____ with _____ that

   _____

5. Wisdom is a/an _____ with _____

   that _____

6. Fear is a/an _____ with _____ that

   _____

Choose one of your metaphors to read to the class.

Responding to the Poem

Emily Dickinson describes hope as a thing with feathers. How would you describe hope? Choose one of the following topics to write about:

1. A time in your life when hope was very important
2. Your hopes for the future
3. Your own description of hope

Write a paragraph.

You Be the Editor

The following restaurant review contains eleven mistakes. Find the mistakes and correct them. Then copy the review onto a separate sheet of paper.

Antonio Guiliani has just opened another of his remarkably wonderful restaurants. He has called this one *Trattoria a Aldo* and located it in the heart of downtown at 141 Main Street. Chef Gianni Forno is known for his fabulous Italian specialties, and this restaurant serve them all. The food here is beautifully prepared served and presented. If you like seafood try the mussels marinara, the fried calamari, or the lobster ravioli. If you like spicy dishes, try the tiny pacific clams sautéed with hot peppers, garlic and white wine. Meat-eaters have a choice between tender, beautiful veal dishes with smooths and lights sauces and hearty beef dishes that are marinated and grilled. This is the place to go for the best homemade pasta in city. The portions are generous, and the sauces are delicious my personal favorite is the "salsa cruda," a sauce made with red onions, black olives, basil, and tomatoes. There is a long list of elaborate pastries on the dessert list. My dining partner chose the chocolate cannoli and I chose the tiramisu. Neither of us were disappointed. Even the bill here was reasonable. With this restaurant, Guiliani has another winner.

—by John Russell

On Your Own

1. Look at the two cartoons below. Choose one and write your reaction to the ideas expressed in the cartoon.

Drawing by Rini, © 1995 *The New Yorker* Magazine, Inc.

2. Write a reaction to a song, TV program, or movie. You may choose one that you are familiar with or one that you have just seen or heard for the first time. Try to bring your own life experiences to your reaction.

Writing Essays for Undergraduate and Graduate School Applications

If you are planning to apply to undergraduate or graduate school in the United States, you will probably have to write a personal essay as part of the application process. Some schools will give you very structured questions and others will give you more open-ended questions. In this chapter, you will practice writing answers to typical application essay questions.

Tips for Writing Application Essays

1. **Take the essay part of the application very seriously.** To some schools, the essay is the most important part of your application. Admissions officers at more than one school have said that the essay can make or break a candidate's chances for admission.

2. **Be honest. Be yourself. Be sincere.** The admissions committees want to know who you are as a person. Do not misrepresent yourself.

3. **Write about something that is important to you.** Even if you are given a specific subject to write about, you will have to choose your angle. Let your enthusiasm for the subject show. Your interest in the subject is a very important, sometimes the most important, element in an essay.

4. **Make your application as interesting and lively as you can.** Admissions officers read hundreds, maybe thousands, of essays. You want yours to stand out.

5. **Do not try to write the application essay in a hurry or at the last minute.** You need to give yourself time to think about the question and do some prewriting and planning before you actually write the essay.

6. **Keep your audience and your purpose in mind as you plan and write your essay.**

7. **Pay attention to the principles of good writing that you have studied in this book.** Think about unity, cohesion, and organization. Include specific details so that your essay is uniquely about you. Do not write an essay that is so general that it could have been written by any number of other people. Add details to bring your essay to life.

8. **Follow the rules you have learned in this book for writing a good introduction, body, and conclusion.**

9. **Your essay must be as perfect as you can make it.** This means no grammatical, spelling, punctuation, or capitalization mistakes. Have several people—teachers, relatives, and/or friends—proofread it carefully for you. Remember that neatness counts.

10. **Make a copy of your essay before you mail it.** This will avoid problems if your application gets lost in the mail or in the admissions office. To be safe, send it registered mail with a return receipt requested.

Whether you are applying to undergraduate or graduate school, there are several principles that you should pay attention to in writing your essays. Even if you are not planning to attend an American university, you will improve your writing skills by practicing this kind of essay.

Undergraduate Essays

The application essay is very important to admissions committees. They use it to get to know the individual behind the test scores and grade point average. You should think of your essay as a chance to show yourself off to your best advantage. Try to tell them a little more about yourself than they would know by reading the rest of your application. Admissions committees also use the essay to determine how well you write because good writing skills are important for success in college. In short, your essay is your special opportunity to prove that you are an interesting person and that you can write well.

Analyzing an Undergraduate Essay

Here is an example of an essay that was written in response to a university's statement, *"In reading your application we want to get to know you as well as we can. We ask that you use this opportunity to tell us something more about yourself that would help us toward a sense of who you are, how you think, and what issues and ideas interest you the most."*

Read the essay and answer the questions that follow.

　　Scuba diving has never been easy for me. When I was in fifth grade, the father of one of my classmates died in a scuba-diving accident. His death, along with the scenes I had watched in James Bond movies of men left to drown hundreds of feet under water with severed air tubes, did not give me the impression that scuba diving was a safe sport. However, in eighth grade, my father asked me if I would take scuba-diving classes with him. Although I was reluctant, the important fact was that he would be there to support me and that we would do it together. It seemed that as I grew older, we spent less time together. I wanted this opportunity to be with him.

　　After hours of pool work and classes, I was ready to go for my certification. My first problem was getting to the dive site. I have a slight fear of boats, which probably stems from my first boat ride, during which I developed a major case of seasickness. This was a small obstacle compared to what

(continued on next page)

was about to come. I spent the first fifteen minutes of the dive standing on the rocking deck of the dive boat, staring at the rough ocean, weak with fear. I was only able to dive into the water after a good pep talk from both my father and my dive master. I repeated the word "relax" to myself over and over and plunged in.

Even now, after five years of scuba diving, I still feel a little uneasy before submerging. However, once I have taken a deep breath and broken the surface of the water, curiosity and astonishment at the variety on the ocean floor calm my apprehensions. There are no sounds or disturbances to break the perfect tranquillity. Enormous purple fans wave in the current, and orange and red sponges jut out of the coral like poppies in a meadow. When I am underwater, I can hover above the colorful, craggy coral, flying like Superman, watching schools of fish dart around in search of food, oblivious to my presence. Underwater, I am able to leave behind my worries and observe the peaceful beauty of nature.

The experience does not end with my surfacing, but continues with the stories my father, the other divers, and I tell afterward. There is a high level of camaraderie among all divers. We sit around like old pirates in a dank tavern, laughing as we talk about the stingrays who search for food in our hair, (an experience that was once described as "like being mugged by E. T.") or about the dive master who found a bicycle down by one of the wrecks and started to ride it around. My fellow divers do not know that I have not yet left behind my fears of diving, because once I submerge, I inhabit a different world with them.

Like learning to scuba dive, learning to read was also not easy for me. Most early-reading programs rèly heavily on the teaching of phonetics. However, I have a learning disability that makes understanding sound/symbol relationships difficult. This made learning to read through the use of phonetics impossible. I was lucky, though, because I was accepted into Fenn School's Intensive Language Program. For two years (fourth and fifth grades), six other boys and I worked together, learning how to compensate for our learning differences. In this class, I developed a trait that I am very proud of: hard work—not only in my studies, but in everything I do.

By continuing even when the waters were rough, and drawing on the support of my parents and teachers, I learned to read and found an amazing world opened to me. Just as my fellow divers do not know that I am anxious about scuba diving, most of my classmates do not know that I have a learning disability. They just think that I am a diligent worker, but I know that, as with scuba diving, there is a lot more to the story.

1. What two experiences did the student write about? How are they related? What was his purpose in talking about scuba diving?

_____

_____

_____

2. What did you learn about this student? What adjectives would you use to describe him?

_____

_____

_____

3. What does the essay reveal about the author's relationship with his father? His value system?

_____

_____

_____

Sample Essay Questions

The most common application essay is the one that asks you for autobiographical information. Some schools ask for it directly with questions such as, "Tell us a little about yourself," or "Give the admissions committee information about yourself that is not included elsewhere on the application." Other schools ask the question indirectly with such questions as, "What person has influenced you most in life?"

Here are some typical essay topics that are often used by colleges and universities in the United States. In small groups, discuss the topics and make notes about how you might answer each one.

1. Evaluate a significant experience or achievement that has special meaning to you.
2. Discuss some issue of personal, local, or national concern and its importance to you.
3. Indicate a person who has had a significant influence on you and describe that influence.
4. What one word best describes you and why?
5. If you could change any event in history, what would you change and why?
6. Describe the most difficult thing that you have ever done.
7. What book has affected you most and why?
8. Describe a change that you have gone through and how it may affect your future.

Writing an Essay for an Undergraduate Application

a. Prewriting
Choose three of the essay topics above and freewrite about each one for ten minutes.

b. Planning
Reread your three freewriting samples and choose one of them to develop into an essay. Using the ideas you generated in your prewriting, prepare an informal outline of the essay.

c. Drafting
On a separate piece of paper, write the first draft of your essay. Be sure to start with an interesting introduction that will make the admissions committee excited about reading your essay. You should choose a pattern of organization for your body paragraphs that best suits your topic. Include specific details and examples that will help the committee get to know you. Finally, make your conclusion one that the readers will remember.

d. Revising
Use the principles on page 54 to revise the first draft. Be sure that all your paragraphs are unified and coherent. Write or type a revised version of your essay.

e. Editing
Use the checklist on page 65 to edit your essay. Correct all the grammar, punctuation, capitalization, and spelling errors. Give your essay to your teacher and someone else to read for any final comments before you copy it over or type it.

 You Be the Editor

Most applications also include several short-answer questions. Do not be deceived by these questions. They are just as important as the longer essay questions, and the same principles apply.

Read the following student response to the short-answer question, "Tell us about the academic areas that interest you most." There are seven mistakes. Find and correct the mistakes.

> I am interested in mathematic and science, but at this point I have not yet identified a specific area to major in. I am also interest in learning more about the field of engineering. At Blake University I can to explore all of these areas, before I decide upon a major. Blake even offer the opportunity to combine them into an interdisciplinary major. finally, although I do not intend to major in art, I have a strong interest in art and find the possible of taking courses at Blake's School of Design attractive.

Filling Out an Application

Many colleges and universities in the United States use the same application form. It is called the *common application.* Turn to the appendix on pages 146 and 147 to see a sample common application from several years ago. Just for practice, take the time to fill it out completely. Make sure that your information is accurate and your handwriting neat and legible.

Graduate School Essays

The biggest difference between essays for undergraduate and graduate school is in the subject matter. A graduate school essay focuses on career goals and is generally referred to as a *statement of purpose.* The principles that you read on page 138 remain the same.

Analyzing a Graduate School Statement of Purpose

Here is an example of a successful graduate school statement of purpose. This student wants to study civil engineering at the University of Michigan.

"Statement of Purpose: (Type or print clearly on a separate piece of paper.) Your statement of purpose should be a concise, well-written essay about your background, your career goals, and how Michigan's graduate program will help you meet your career and educational objectives."

Read the essay and answer the questions that follow.

My lifelong passion for structures and construction was sparked in 1978 when I got my first LEGO™ set. I would spend hours imagining and drawing buildings and bridges and trying to make them out of LEGOs™. My father is a civil engineer, and one of my greatest joys was accompanying him to oversee the progress at his construction sites. There was nothing more intriguing to me then than watching a structure transform from a sketch on an engineer's pad to a building in our community. I can still remember the sense of pride I felt upon the completion of the dam my father had engineered. Ever since I was a child, my dream has been to become a civil engineer and join my father in his company. Over the years, my dream has not changed, but the path to my goal has become more complicated. As I watched Turkey go through a series of political and economic changes, I felt the great effect it had on companies like my father's. I came to realize that in order to be a successful civil engineer, I would need to acquire a diversity of skills.

When I was in high school, the Turkish economy was tightly held in the hands of the government. Almost all major industries were dominated by government monopolies, leaving little room for the private sector to flourish. Then, seemingly overnight, Turkey went from an economy based on small family businesses and government-held industries to a competitive market modeled on the Western style. The privatization of Turkish industries in the late 1980s and a concurrent influx of foreign investments led to the birth of big corporations in all industries, including construction. However, the transition has not always been a smooth one. Turkey lacked a solid core of educated business professionals capable of dealing with the rapid economic growth that involved newly defined business relations at corporate levels. There was only a handful of Turkish business people skilled at negotiating with managers of foreign companies.

Realizing this need, I decided that the first step of my educational plan should be to study business and finance at an American university. This would provide me with the solid foundation of knowledge and skills that I would need in my construction management career. When I left home in 1989 to come to the United States, Turkey was on the brink of a new era. During the five years that I have been here completing my undergraduate education, Turkey has undergone tremendous changes in all spheres: political, social, economic, and technological. Old systems and traditional models were replaced with contemporary ones as Western influences became more dominant.

During the past five years, I have become fluent in English while earning a bachelor of science degree in finance, with a minor in economics. I am currently completing a second bachelor's degree in mathematics. Now, I will further my education by pursuing graduate studies in civil engineering. Turkey's recent economic boom has brought an unprecedented wave of unmanaged construction in urban areas, revealing a need for highly trained engineers with managerial skills. The Construction Engineering and Management program at the University of Michigan will expand upon my present management knowledge and train me in the engineering skills necessary to plan, coordinate, and control the diverse range of specialists involved in the construction industry. I feel that my background in economics and finance, coupled with my strong quantitative skills, makes me an excellent candidate for graduate studies in this field.

(continued on next page)

Michigan's Construction Engineering and Management program will prepare me for a responsible management position in the construction industry. At Michigan, I hope to be involved in research that investigates the applications of artificial intelligence techniques as well as computer applications in the construction industry. I would also like to research strategies for innovation in construction, especially as they relate to a developing country. Finally, I am interested in how the planning, design, and implementation of engineering projects are integrated into a coherent, well-functioning system. I hope to improve my understanding of the whole system by examining how the subsystems and various components fit together.

Since one of my goals is to improve the operation and management of Turkey's present inefficient infrastructure, I would like to study ways of improving efficiency in the use of labor and natural resources. This will involve rebuilding, restoring, and upgrading a rapidly deteriorating infrastructure as well as creating new physical structures that reflect the application of modern technology. Turkey desperately needs new airports, harbors, highways, public transportation systems, and industrial plants to facilitate its rapid economic growth. The engineering problems Turkey faces require professionals who are able to bring together ideas from technology, science, and systems and operations management.

By earning an M.S. degree in construction engineering and management, I will return to Turkey equipped with the most sophisticated knowledge in my field. I hope not only to learn practical information that I can apply to the situation in Turkey, but also to acquire the theoretical basis and research skills necessary to identify structural, managerial, and economic problems and formulate strategies for solutions. My ultimate goal is to be a professional with the ability to implement my vision for the future of Turkey.

1. What did this essay tell you about the student's background?

   _____

   _____

   _____

2. Why do you think the student mentioned playing with LEGOs™ in the introduction?

   _____

   _____

   _____

3. Why is the student interested in studying engineering?

   _____

   _____

   _____

4. What experiences led him to this interest?

   _____

   _____

   _____

5. How has he prepared himself for graduate school?

_____

_____

_____

6. What qualities do you detect about this student that will make him successful in graduate school?

_____

_____

_____

Writing a Statement of Purpose

Practice writing a statement of purpose. Respond to the following sample question:

"In the space below, please discuss your educational background, career objectives, and research interests. Be as specific as you can about the area in which you plan to study."

a. Prewriting
Choose one of the prewriting techniques that you are comfortable with. Use the space below to generate ideas.

b. Planning
Organize your prewriting.

c. Drafting
On a separate piece of paper, write the first draft of your essay.

d. Revising
Use the principles on page 54 to revise the first draft. Be sure that all your paragraphs are unified and coherent. Write or type a revised version of your essay.

e. Editing
Use the checklist on page 65 to edit your essay. Correct all the grammar, punctuation, capitalization, and spelling errors. Give your essay to your teacher and someone else to read for any final comments before you copy it over or type it.

Appendix

APPLICATION FOR UNDERGRADUATE ADMISSION

PERSONAL DATA

Legal name: _____
    Last   *First*   *Middle (complete)*   *Jr., etc.*   *Sex*

Prefer to be called: _____ (nickname)   Former last name(s) if any: _____

Are you applying as a ☐ freshman or ☐ transfer student?   For the term beginning: _____

Permanent home address: _____
            Number and Street

_____
    City or Town   *County*   *State*   *Zip*

If different from the above, please give your mailing address for all admission correspondence:

Mailing address: _____
            Number and Street

_____ Use until: _____
    City or Town   *State*   *Zip*   *Date*

Telephone at mailing address: _____/_____   Permanent home telephone: _____/_____
    Area Code   *Number*   *Area Code*   *Number*

Birthdate: _____ Citizenship: ☐ U.S. ☐ Permanent Resident U.S. ☐ Other _____ Visa type _____
    Month *Day* *Year*   *Country*

Possible area(s) of academic concentration/major: _____ or undecided ☐

Special college or division if applicable: _____

Possible career or professional plans: _____ or undecided ☐

Will you be a candidate for financial aid? ☐ Yes ☐ No If yes, the appropriate form(s) was/will be filed on: _____

The following items are optional: Social Security number, if any: ☐ ☐ ☐ – ☐ ☐ – ☐ ☐ ☐ ☐

Place of birth: _____ Marital status: _____
    City   *State*   *Country*

First language, if other than English: _____ Language spoken at home: _____

How would you describe yourself? Check any that apply.

☐ American Indian, Alaskan Native (tribal affiliation _____)   ☐ Mexican American, Mexican

☐ Native Hawaiian, Pacific Islander   ☐ African American, Black

☐ Asian American, Asian (including Indian subcontinent) (country _____)   ☐ White, Anglo, Caucasian

☐ Hispanic, Latino (including Puerto Rican) (country _____)   ☐ Other (Specify_____)

EDUCATIONAL DATA

School you attend now _____ Date of entry _____

Address _____ ACT/CEEB code number _____
    City   *State*   *Zip Code*

Date of secondary graduation _____ Is your school public? _____ private? _____ parochial? _____

College counselor: Name: _____ Position: _____

School telelephone: _____/_____   School FAX: _____/_____
    Area Code   *Number*   *Area Code*   *Number*   **APP**

ACADEMIC HONORS

Briefly describe any scholastic distinctions or honors you have won beginning with ninth grade:

_____

_____

_____

EXTRACURRICULAR, PERSONAL, AND VOLUNTEER ACTIVITIES

Please list your principal extracurricular, community, and family activities and hobbies in the order of their interest to you. Include specific events and/or major accomplishments such as musical instrument played, varsity letters earned, etc. Please (✓) in the right column those activities you hope to pursue in college.

Activity	Grade level or post-secondary (p.s.) 9 10 11 12 PS	Approximate time spent — Hours per week	Weeks per year	Positions held, honors won, or letters earned	Do you plan to participate in college?

WORK EXPERIENCE

List any job (including summer employment) you have held during the past three years.

Specific nature of work	Employer	Approximate dates of employment	Approximate no. of hours spent per week

In the space provided below, briefly discuss which of these activities (extracurricular and personal activities or work experience) has had the most meaning for you, and why.

_____

_____

_____

_____

_____

_____

ANSWER KEY

Answers for Chapters 1 and 2 will vary.

Chapter 3
Chapter Highlights

Chapter 4
You Be the Editor

Here is one possible corrected version. The paragraph can be corrected in more than one way.

How could I have been so stupid? I let my car run out of gas on the interstate just when I was in a hurry to get to work on time. There was no gas station in sight and no hope, unless I got lucky and a kind person with a car phone came along, saw me sitting there, and called for help. Guess what! That's what happened! I was only twenty minutes late for work. It would have been more if that nice man hadn't come along.

You Be the Editor

Wall Street is a narrow, winding street that is less than one Mile long. Despite the fact that ○ is a tiny street, Wall Street is one of the most influential and best-known streets in the world. To most people, Wall Street is synonymous with the New York Stock Exchange and the world of stocks ○ bonds ○ and securities. Because of its location on a thriving and busy harbor at the southern tip of manhattan island. The Wall Street area has historically been an important area for business and trade. It's convenient location made its growth as a center of finance natural. Over the years, Wall Street has become an international symbol of power and high finance. Its name brings to mind power and the excitement of the stock market ○ and its economic, political, and personal impact is felt daily by millions of people all over the world.

Chapter 5

You Be the Editor

If you like to eat or bake delicious cookies, you will love this recipe. Soften ¹/₂ pound of butter and mix it together with 2 cups of (f) sugar. Stir in 3 beaten egg○ and 9 table-spoons of lemon juice. Then add 4 cups of flour ○ 1 teaspoon of baking powder ○ and 2–¹/₂ teaspoons of nutmeg. As soon as the mixture is thoroughly combined, form the dough into a large ball and refrigerat(or) it for at least 1 hour. When you are ready to bake the cookies, divide the ball of dough in half. Roll the dough out so that ○ is ¹/₈ inch thick. It will be easier if you use a rolling pin. Cut the cookies into shapes, using the open end of a glass or cookie cutters if you have them. Put the cookies on greased cookie sheets and bake them at 375 degrees for 6 minutes. To make them sweeter and more festive, frost them with colored frosting. With this recipe, the hardest part is try-ing not to eat to○ many!

Chapter 6

You Be the Editor

Consumer products are usually divided into three categories○ convenience, shop-ping, and specialty products. Each category is based on the way people buy(s) products. Convenience products are products that a consumer needs but that he or she is not will-ing to spend very much time or effort shopping for. Convenience products ○ usually inexpensive, frequently purchased items. Some common examples are bread, newspa-pers ○ soda, and gasoline. Buyers spend (few) time planning the purchase of a convenience product. (A)lso do not compare brands or sellers. The second category, shopping products, are those products that customers feel are worth the time and effort to compare with competing products. Furniture, refrigerators, cars, and televisions are examples of shopping products. Because these products are expected to last a long time(T)hey are purchased less frequently than convenience products. The last catego-ry is specialty products. Specialty products are consumer products that the customer really wants and makes a special effort to find and buy(ing). Buyers actually plan the purchase of a specialty product. They know what they want and will not accept a sub-stitute. Fancy photographic equipment and a haircut by a certain stylist are examples of specialty products. In searching for specialty products(. B)uyers do not compare alternatives.

Chapter 7

You Be the Editor

The Great Depression of the 1930s affected Americans for generations. The complete collapse of the stock market began on October 24 ○ 1929, when 13 million shares of stock were sold. On Tuesday, October 29, known as Black Tuesday, more than 16 million shares were sold. The value of most shares fell sharply, resulting in financial ruin and widespread panic. Although there have been other financial panics(N)one has had such a devastating and long-term effect as the Great Depression. By 1932, the industri-al output of the (u)nited (s)tates had been cut in half. One-fourth of the labor force, about 15 million people, was out of work, and hourly wages dropped almost 50 percent. In addition, hundreds of banks (will fail). Prices for agricultural products dropped to their lowest level since the Civil War. More than 90,000 businesses failed complete○. Statistics, however, cannot tell the story of the extraordinary hardships the masses of (a)mericans suffered. For nearly every unemployed (people), there were dependents who needed to be fed and housed. People in the United States had never known such massive poverty and hunger before. Former millionaires stood on street corners trying to sell○ apples at 5 cents apiece. Thousands (lose) their homes(. B)ecause they could

(continued on next page)

not pay their mortgages. Some people moved in with relatives. Others moved to shabby sections of town and built shelters out of tin cans and cardboard. Homeless people slept outside under old newspapers. Many Americans waited in lines in every city, hoping for something to eat. Unfortunately, many of these people died of malnutrition. In 1931 alone, more than 20,000 Americans committed suicide.

Chapter 8

You Be the Editor

Now that I am pregnant with our first child, my husband and I will have to find a bigger place to live. Our little apartment in the city is too small for three people. We ○ trying to decide whether we should get a bigg(est) apartment in the city or move to the suburbs. We have four main considerations ○ expense, space, convenience, and schools. In general, ○ is probably (expensiver) to live in the city. On the other hand, we would have to buy a car if we moved to the suburbs (w)e would also have to buy a lawnmower and a snowblower or hire someone ○ care for the lawn and driveway. In terms of space, we could definitely have a bigger house and much more land if we lived in the suburbs. However, we wonder if it would be worth it, since we would lose so many conveniences. Stores would be farther away and so would friends, neighbors, movie theaters, museums, and restaurants. The (most) biggest inconvenience would be that we would both have to commute to work every day instead of walking or taking the bus. The (S)chools are probably better in the suburbs, but for our child, who isn't even born yet, school is several years away. In looking at our priorities, it becomes clear that we should continue to live in the city for now and then reevaluate our decision as the baby gets closer to school age.

Chapter 9

You Be the Editor

If you are like most people, you average one to three colds per year. Even if you do not have a cold right now (. T)he chances are three in four that within the next year, at least one cold virus will find you. (t)hen you'll spend a week or so suffering from the miseries of the common cold: fatigue, sore throat, laryngitis, sneezing, stuffy or runny nose, and coughing. According to researchers, colds are the most common medical reason for missing school and work. Once you catch a cold, what can you do⊙ There is no known cure yet for a cold. There are, however, several thing○ you can do to suppress the symptom(')s so that you feel better while the virus runs its course. For example, make sure that you get plenty of sleep and drink lots of liquids. You may find commercially available cold remedies such as decongestants, cough suppressants, and expectorants helpful, but keep in mind that these products can cause side effects. Many people prefer home remedies such as chicken soup, garlic, and ginger tea. In treating a cold, remember the wisdom of the ages, "(i)f you treat a cold, it will be gone in a week; if you don't treat it, ○ will be gone in seven days."

Chapter 10

You Be the Editor

Dear Helene,

   I just finished reading one of the best books I have ever read. It is called <u>One Hundred Years of Solitude</u> and was written by Gabriel García Márquez. He won the Nobel Prize for this book in 1982. It was first published in 1967 in Argentina and translated into Ⓔnglish in 1970. Briefly, it is the story of the fictional town of Macondo as seen through the eyes of many generations of the Buendía family. We learn about the changes that the town goes through as it grow◯ and the years roll by ⟨we⟩ also read about the universal themes of birth, death, love, war, wealth, poverty, honor ◯ and corruption as we spend time with this large and fascinating family. The writing is simple, yet beautiful, even in translation. If you are looking for a really good book to read, ◯ recommend this book to you. Let me know if you read it. I hope that you enjoy reading about these people and their lives as much as I did.

Love,

Judy

Chapter 11

You Be the Editor

   Antonio Guiliani has just opened another of his remarkably wonderful restaurants. He has called this one *Trattoria a Aldo* and located it in the heart of downtown at 141 Main Street. Chef Gianni Forno is known for his fabulous Italian specialties, and this restaurant serve◯ them all. The food here is beautifully prepared ◯ served ◯ and presented. If you like seafood ◯ try the mussels marinara, the fried calamari, or the lobster ravioli. If you like spicy dishes, try the tiny Ⓟacific clams sautéed with hot peppers, garlic ◯ and white wine. Meat-eaters have a choice between tender, beautiful veal dishes with smoothⓈ and lightⓈ sauces and hearty beef dishes that are marinated and grilled. This is the place to go for the best homemade pasta in ◯ city. The portions are generous, and the sauces are delicious ⟨m⟩y personal favorite is the "salsa cruda," a sauce made with red onions, black olives, basil, and tomatoes. There is a long list of elaborate pastries on the dessert list. My dining partner chose the chocolate cannoli and I chose the tiramisu. Neither of us ⟨were⟩ disappointed. Even the bill here was reasonable. With this restaurant, Guiliani has another winner.

Chapter 12

You Be the Editor

   I am interested in mathematic◯ and science, but at this point I have not yet identified a specific area to major in. I am also interest◯ in learning more about the field of engineering. At Blake University I can ⟨to⟩ explore all of these areas◯ before I decide upon a major. Blake even offer◯ the opportunity to combine them into an interdisciplinary major. Ⓕinally, although I do not intend to major in art, I have a strong interest in art and find the ⟨possible⟩ of taking courses at Blake's School of Design attractive.

Credits

page 6. From *Dave Barry's Only Travel Guide You'll Ever Need,* by Dave Barry, Fawcett Columbine Books, New York, 1991, pp. 19, 20.

page 23. Source: *Dos and Taboos Around the World,* edited by Roger Axtell, John Wiley and Sons, New York, 1993.

page 23. Source: *Encarta* 1994, "Pets." Microsoft.

page 32. Source: *Car and Travel,* "Seven Stress-Busters for Air Travelers," by Anne Kelleher, Nov.–Dec. 1995, pp. 8–9.

page 34. From Carol Varley and Lisa Miles, *The USBORNE Geography Encyclopedia,* E.D.C. Publishers, Tulsa, Oklahoma, p. 24.

page 40. "John Lennon: A Musician for All Time" by Leslie Leibowitz. Reprinted with permission.

page 43. From "Pet Therapy," Sy Montgomery, *Cobblestone,* June 1985, p. 21.

page 49. From "Sleeping Well", Nick Gallo, *Your Health and Fitness,* p. 7.

page 50. Source: *Conde Nast Traveler,* "How Safe Is Flying?" by Gary Stoller, Dec. 1995, pp. 116–118.

page 50. From "I Won't Go Quietly," by Michael Elliott and Daniel Pedersen, *Newsweek,* December 4, 1995, p. 66.

page 73. Sources: *Psychology,* 2d ed., Diane E. Papalia, Sally W. Olds, McGraw-Hill Book Co., New York, 1988, p. 175. *Cat Catalog,* edited by Judy Firemen, "How to Teach Your Cat to Shake Hands," by Ken Von Der Porten, Workman Publishing Co., New York, 1976, pp. 289–290. *Introduction to Psychology,* 11th ed., Rita Atkinson, Richard Atkinson, Edward Smith, and Daryl Bem, Harcourt Brace College Publishers, New York, 1993, p. 267.

page 81. "The Marketing Mix" by Josh Rothbard. Reprinted with permission.

page 90. Sources: *World Book Encyclopedia,* 1989, Volume D, #5, p. 218, "Dinosaur" by Peter Dodson. *The Evolution Book,* Sara Stern, Workman Publishing Co., Inc., New York, 1986, pp. 227–228.

page 99. Sources: "The 'Jim' Twins" by Betty Springer, *Good Housekeeping,* February 1980, pp. 123, 206, 208, 210. "Double Mystery" by Lawrence Wright, *New Yorker,* August 7, 1995, pp. 49–50.

page 112. "Energy Sources: A Dilemma for the 21st century" by Alan Bronstein. Reprinted with permission.

page 115. Source: *Jane Brody's Cold and Flu Fighter,* Jane Brody, W. W. Norton Company, New York, 1995.

page 117. From *Boys' Life,* "The Growing of Green Cars" by W. E. Butterworth IV, May 1993, pp. 44–47. Reprinted with permission.

page 119. From *Boston Globe,* Jan 18, 1996. Reprinted courtesy of *Boston Globe.*

page 122. "Politics As Usual" by Diana Childress. From *Cobblestone*'s April 1995 issue: *Franklin D. Roosevelt,* © 1995, Cobblestone Publishing, Inc., 7 School St., Peterborough, NH 03458. Reprinted by permission of the publisher.

page 124. Sources: "He Was in a League of His Own," Bob Ryan, *Boston Globe,* August 19, 1992, pp. 1, 71. "Last Flight of a Legend," *Time,* August 16, 1992, p. 21. *Washington Monthly,* book review by Jonathan Rowe of *Larry Bird: The Making of an American Sports Legend,* by Daniel Levine, May 1989, pp. 55–56.

page 133. "The Road Not Taken" from *The Poetry of Robert Frost,* Heny Holt and Company, Inc., New York, 1916. Reprinted by permission of the publisher.

page 135. "Hope Is the Thing with Feathers" by Emily Dickinson. Reprinted courtesy of Harvard University Press.

page 139. "Taking the Plunge" by Matthew Root. Reprinted with permission.

page 143. Statement of Purpose for graduate school essay by Hasan Halkali. Reprinted with permission.